The Blackdown Hills landscape

A landscape assessment
prepared for the Countryside Commission
by Cobham Resource Consultants

Countryside
COMMISSION

Published by:
Countryside Commission
John Dower House
Crescent Place
Cheltenham GL50 3RA
© Countryside Commission 1989

Distributed by:
Countryside Commission Publications
19/23 Albert Road
Manchester M19 2EQ
CCP 258
Price: £5.00

Contents

Figures

British Library Cataloguing in Publication Data
The Blackdown Hills landscape: a landscape assessment
1. England. Areas of outstanding natural beauty
I. Cobham Resource Consultants
719'.0942
ISBN 0 86170 212 3

Designed and produced by CGS Studios - Cheltenham.
Printed by Cotswold Printing Company - Stroud.

Foreword

The Blackdown Hills are a comparatively little known group of hills lying on the borders of Devon and Somerset south of Taunton. Broadly, the area extends from Wellington in the north to Honiton in the south; from Cullompton in the west to Chard in the east.

In 1947 the Blackdown Hills were included in a wider area — the Blackdown Hills and Sidmouth Bay Conservation Area — recommended by the National Parks Committee [1], under the chairmanship of Sir Arthur Hobhouse, for potential designation as an area of outstanding natural beauty (AONB). Subsequently, priority was given to the designation of coastal AONBs, and the Sidmouth Bay area alone was designated as the East Devon AONB in 1963.

The Countryside Commission recently asked Cobham Resource Consultants, as independent consultants, to prepare an assessment of the landscape character and quality of the Blackdown Hills. Whilst the views expressed are those of the consultants, we are now publishing the assessment as a contribution to the understanding and public awareness of this beautiful area, which we believe to be of national importance and therefore worthy of recognition through AONB designation.

Sir Derek Barber
Chairman
Countryside Commission

Preface

In preparing our assessment we have asked ourselves two questions about the meaning of the AONB designation.

First, what does 'natural beauty' consist of? We have been guided by the definition of natural beauty given in the Wildlife and Countryside Act 1981 [2] and by the Countryside Commission's own interpretation of natural beauty [3]. We conclude that, although the emphasis should be on visual quality, geology, topography, flora, fauna, historical and cultural aspects are also relevant.

Second, and perhaps more important, in what way must an AONB be outstanding? The answer — according to Countryside Commission AONB policy [4] — is that it should be of such fine landscape quality that there is a national as well as a local interest in its conservation. This implies that it should have features that are not only distinctive, but also unusual or even unique. It also suggests that these features should be highly valued, not just by landscape specialists, but also by the general public, among whom there should be a broad consensus as to the area's importance and beauty.

These considerations have guided us in the preparation of the landscape assessment, for which we have adopted the approach recommended by the Countryside Commission in its document *Landscape Assessment: A Countryside Commission Approach* [3].

We begin by describing the area factually, in terms of its physical features and history, and its visual, ecological and architectural character. Next, we examine how the Blackdown Hills have been perceived through time, by writers and artists, visitors and local residents. We also consider how the landscape is changing, and how it may change in future. Finally we spell out as clearly and simply as possible, the area's essential landscape qualities, based on common sense, the perceptions of others, and our own professional judgement.

For the purpose of this assessment the boundaries of the area are as defined by Hobhouse in 1947.

Acknowledgements

Special thanks are due to Dr Peter Howard, who assisted us in collating material about artists' perceptions of the Blackdown Hills, and Peter Hamilton, who provided all the photographs for this publication.

We are grateful to the following for other illustrative material: Devon Record Office; Royal Albert Memorial Museum, Exeter; Whitworth Art Gallery, University of Manchester; and Ulster Museum.

Thanks are also due to the many organisations and individuals, too numerous to name, who provided us with invaluable information and comment about the landscape of the Blackdown Hills in the course of the study.

The study team: Julie Martin, Jenny Collison, Duncan McInerney and Andy McNab.

Figures 1–3 are based on the Ordnance Survey map, figure 4 also incorporates information supplied by Cobham Resource Consultants.

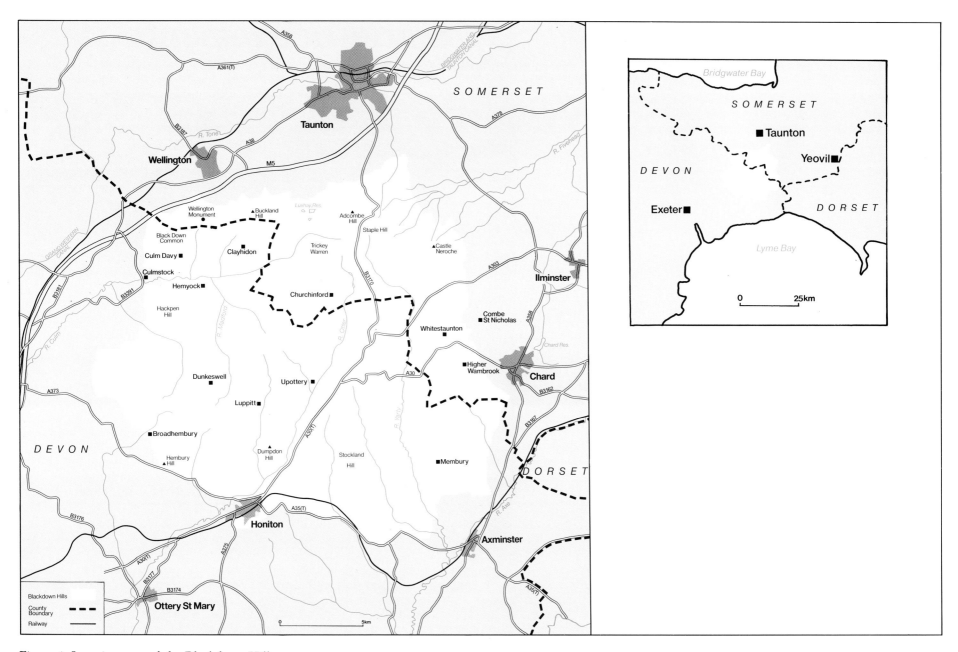

Figure 1. Location map of the Blackdown Hills.

1. The development of the Blackdown Hills landscape

Introduction

The Blackdown Hills (**Figure 1**) are best known for the steep, wooded scarp face they present to the north. To the south the land dips away gently as a plateau, deeply dissected by valleys and combes. On the top of the plateau there are wide, open, windswept spaces; in the valleys nestle villages and hamlets, surrounded by an intricate pattern of small enclosed fields, and linked by a maze of high-hedged lanes. As one travels around the area, the view is constantly changing, from long-distance panoramas to rustic scenes of agricultural and village life.

This great diversity of land form, land use and landscape features can be explained to a considerable extent by the physical and historical influences that have acted upon the landscape through time. The evidence of these forces at work can be seen very clearly in the Blackdown Hills, compared with many other parts of Britain.

Physical influences

The dominant physical influence upon the Blackdown Hills is the underlying geology (**Figure 2**), which is quite different from that of the rest of southern England. The Blackdowns, together with the East Devon AONB, form the only extensive outcrop of Upper Greensand in the region. Moreover, the Greensand of the Blackdowns differs from Greensand elsewhere because it is a thick, massive, largely non-calcareous outcrop containing cherts (siliceous concretions, similar to flint) [5].

Above the Greensand is a thin layer of clay with flints and cherts. In the south-eastern part of the area, around Whitestaunton, chalk also appears above the Greensand in places. Below the Greensand are impermeable rocks, mainly Keuper Marls but also Lower Lias in the east. These strata are exposed in the river valleys. There are drift deposits of gravel and alluvium in all the valleys.

The geology has had a distinct impact on the topography and drainage of the Blackdowns (**Figure 3**), as well as on soils and land use. The most prominent landform is the main linear east – west Greensand ridge (high point Staple Hill, 315m). To the south the Greensand has been eroded into long, finger-like ridges, separated by deep combes. Further south still, the landscape is more gentle, with rolling ridgeland falling away into wide, open valleys.

Around the edges of all the ridges, where the Greensand meets the underlying impermeable rocks, there is a series of spring lines. Here are found the sources of several substantial rivers: the southward flowing Culm, Otter and Yarty, and the northward flowing tributaries of the Somerset rivers Tone and Fivehead.

The Greensand gives rise to relatively poor, slightly acid soils. On the highest ground, where there is a superficial clay capping, there are fine silty loams with a slowly permeable subsoil. The land here is classified as Grade 3 agricultural land; typical usage is cereals, improved grassland and dairying. The clay has also yielded flints and cherts for use as building materials.

On some ridges and down the valley slopes the soils are coarser. There are localised spots of well-drained loamy soils but other areas may be subject to land slip and waterlogging. Waterlogged areas are sometimes characterised by a poorly drained peaty surface horizon. A mixture of heath, moorland, permanent pasture, wetland and woodland are found on these ridges and slopes, which are mainly Grades 4 and 5 agricultural land.

In the river valleys there are fine loams and silts, subject to slight seasonal waterlogging. Typical land uses are dairying and other stock rearing, on Grade 4 land.

Human influences

Human influences on the Blackdown Hills landscape are also very visible to the informed observer, and an understanding of the main factors at work helps to explain the appearance of the landscape today.

Little is known with any certainty about the landscape of the Blackdown Hills in prehistoric times. However, it is likely that the area was originally covered by woodland, dominated by oak. There is archaeological evidence of human habitation from at least the Mesolithic period, about 7000 years ago; indeed the upper Yarty Valley may have been a centre of Mesolithic activity. During the Neolithic period, 4500 – 2000 BC, it is probable that much of the forest was cleared, particularly on the drier high ground, and at this time trackways may have been established along the ridge tops. From the later, Bronze Age period (2400 – 750 BC) numerous round barrows survive, again on high ground. During the Iron Age (750 BC – 40 AD) an impressive series of hill forts was built, including Hembury, Dumpdon and Castle Neroche. These were often large, and characterised by concentric lines of earthwork defences.

The Romans were active in Devon but not to any great extent within the Blackdowns. There are Roman roads, such as the Fosse Way, to the south and east, but only limited evidence of settlement has been uncovered. Later, between the sixth and tenth centuries, the native Celtic population was gradually displaced by Saxon settlement, for instance in the Culm Valley. For the first time the heavier valley soils were cultivated. Villages were established, accompanied originally by an open field system.

A number of hamlets and farmsteads in the Blackdowns are mentioned in Domesday Book, for example Luppitt, Hemyock and Upottery [6]. Domesday Book also draws attention to the Forest of Neroche, which was the biggest concentration of woodland in south-west England at the time. Neroche extended eastwards from the north-east corner of the Blackdowns. At its highest point, the site of the Iron Age hill fort, a Norman motte and bailey castle was constructed overlooking the forest. Throughout the medieval period Neroche was a royal hunting forest of woodland and parkland [7].

Another development in early medieval times was the founding of a Cistercian monastery at Dunkeswell in 1201. The Cistercians usually settled in a wilderness and

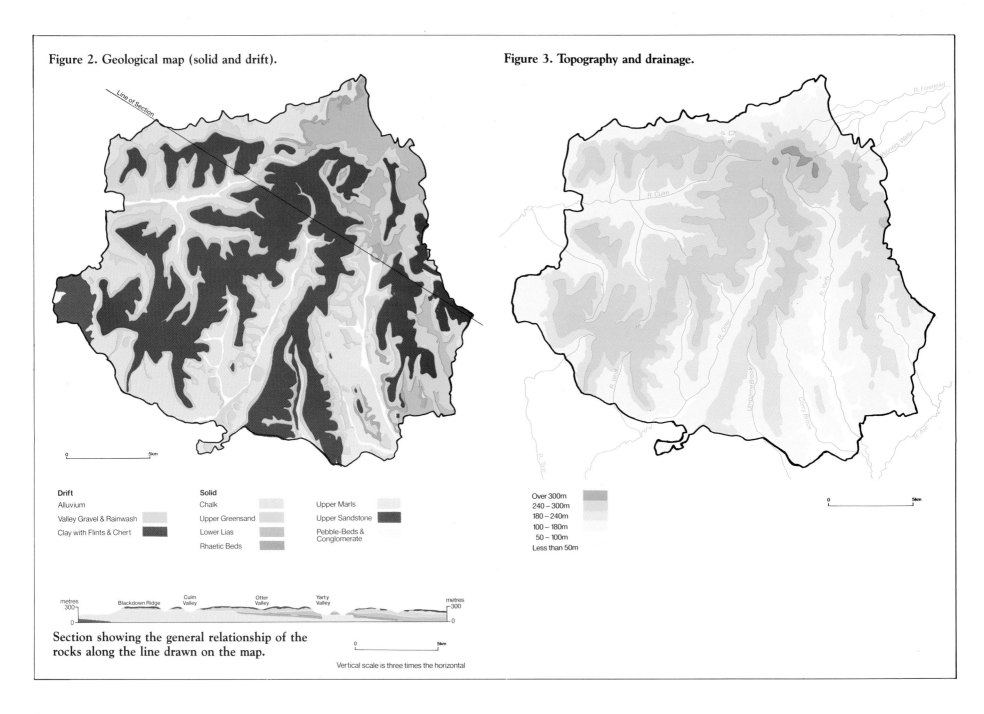

Figure 2. Geological map (solid and drift).

Line of Section

0 — 5km

Drift
Alluvium
Valley Gravel & Rainwash
Clay with Flints & Chert

Solid
Chalk
Upper Greensand
Lower Lias
Rhaetic Beds
Upper Marls
Upper Sandstone
Pebble-Beds & Conglomerate

metres 300 — Blackdown Ridge — Culm Valley — Otter Valley — Yarty Valley — metres 300

Section showing the general relationship of the rocks along the line drawn on the map.

0 — 5km

Vertical scale is three times the horizontal

Figure 3. Topography and drainage.

R. Fivehead
Jenners Water
R. Culm
R. Yarty
R. Otter
R. Wol
Umborne Brook
Corry Brook
R. Tale
R. Axe

Over 300m
240 – 300m
180 – 240m
100 – 180m
50 – 100m
Less than 50m

0 — 5km

The scarp face of the Blackdown Hills, which overlooks the M5 motorway, is the best known feature of the area. Wellington Monument forms a landmark.

The Greensand, which dominates the area geologically, occurs around the edge of all the ridges. In this zone there are steep slopes, and a series of spring lines.

The thin layer of clay with flints and cherts that caps the Greensand on the ridges has yielded chertstone, an unusual building material, here shown as wall, the upper part being cob.

In the valleys and combes of the Blackdowns, a pattern of small, hedged fields was established in medieval times. Much of this pattern survives today.

An impressive series of Iron Age hill forts is found in the Blackdowns. Dumpdon Fort, crowned with trees, is shown here.

In the early nineteenth century the high ridgeland, formerly 'wasteland', was enclosed. A large, regular field pattern was established, for example here, at Stockland Hill.

brought it into cultivation; this seems to have been what happened in the Blackdowns. They acquired much land, cleared woodland and reclaimed moorland to large-scale sheep farming, and established manor and grange farms over a wide area. For example, Broadhembury grange and village were originally in the ownership of Dunkeswell Abbey. Evidence of early settlement can be seen throughout the Blackdowns in the fact that many of the area's buildings date back to the fourteenth and fifteenth centuries. Most of the hamlets and villages are found in the valleys, and were probably settled by 1350. There are also scattered, isolated farmsteads originating from this period.

Perhaps the overriding influence on the pattern of the Blackdown Hills landscape was the enclosures. There were two separate periods of enclosures: the early, medieval enclosures, and the later nineteenth century enclosures [8].

In Somerset and Devon, enclosure of the communal open field system began much sooner than in many other parts of the country. It started with consolidation of holdings, by purchase and exchange. In order to mark the limits of the holder's land, trenches were dug and the soil was thrown up into mounds, which were then planted with hedges. Holdings were subdivided in a similar way to help control grazing and provide shelter for livestock. The small fields, hedges and banks created in this way are now a characteristic feature of the landscape of the south-west.

In the Blackdown Hills it seems that only the valley bottoms and sides were enclosed in medieval times. The higher, more exposed ground remained as commons of woodland, bog, scrub and heath, which provided firewood, turf, bracken for bedding, and upland pasture. There were squatters' rights over this common land, and this meant that enclosures continued on a piecemeal basis up until the eighteenth century. However, because the land was poor the enclosures were often subsequently abandoned, and the remains of some such abandoned farms can still be seen.

The place names of the Blackdown Hills shed further light on the early landscape and land use pattern. One of the most common place name suffixes is 'hayes', which means hedged enclosure. Others are 'cot' or 'cote', meaning outlying farm; 'leigh', meaning clearing in woodland; and 'turbary', meaning a common where turf is cut.

It was not until the nineteenth century that the high ridgeland of the Blackdowns was farmed on a more permanent basis. Together with other 'wastelands' throughout the country, it was subject to parliamentary enclosure acts to bring land into cultivation. These parliamentary enclosures were quite different from the earlier enclosures. The fields were large and regular, the hedges were not so steeply banked, and there were comparatively few hedgerow trees. Wide, straight enclosure roads and turnpikes were built, to minimum standards specified by parliament. Avenues of trees were frequently planted to flank the new roads. Many of these features can still be seen today.

These have been the main influences on the development of the Blackdown Hills landscape. There have been modest changes in the course of the last century (see Chapter 4) but the basic physical and human influences are still very evident. The next chapter goes on to examine the character of the landscape today.

2. The character of the landscape today

In analysing the character of the Blackdown Hills today we have found it helpful to consider the landscape from several different perspectives. Primarily, we have looked on it as a visual resource, and thus its visual character is described in some detail. However, we are also conscious that it is an ecological resource, and that its ecological characteristics may not be immediately obvious to the casual observer. Therefore these too are covered. Finally, we look at the landscape as a human habitat and consider the character of its settlements. Together these three separate 'strands' make up the character of the landscape as a whole.

Visual character

In visual terms, the Blackdowns can be divided into a number of different zones of broadly similar character (**Figure 4**):
- the dramatic northern escarpment of the Blackdown Hills;
- the softer, wooded ridge at the eastern end of the northern escarpment;
- the flat, upland plateau land that lies between the Culm and Otter Valleys;
- the long fingers of rolling ridgeland that spring from the northern escarpment and upland plateau;
- the river valleys of the Culm, Otter, Yarty and Fivehead, each of which have slightly differing characters while sharing the same dominant features.

The northern escarpment

This is an east – west ridge with a dramatically steep and well-wooded northern escarpment. Its essentially linear topography is emphasised by the straight road running along the top of the ridge. On a high bluff overlooking the steep slopes the Wellington Monument is a prominent landmark.

Land use along the ridge is varied. There are enclaves of small flat fields surrounded by neat, wedge-shaped hedgebanks with isolated and windswept hedgerow trees. On Leigh Hill there is a small but distinctive open area of improved sheep pasture, delineated by fences and sheltered by two bands of Scots pine. Elsewhere the deciduous woodland growing on the slopes closes in across the ridge, enclosing small grassland fields surrounded by banks and half-laid hedgerows.

To the north the escarpment falls away sharply into a vast, lowland plain outside the study area, dominated by the M5 motorway, the town of Wellington and all the infrastructure associated with a well-populated area. Looking back up the scarp, patches of bracken, gorse and scrub on the crest give way to dense beech, oak and pine woodland on the steep upper slopes. As the incline progressively lessens there are small, marshy fields bounded by banks of scrubby ash and hazel; further still down the slope the fields become larger and the hedges neater. The gently rolling contours of the lower slopes are regularly incised by dry valleys and small streams edged with alder. It is a complex and colourful landscape containing few buildings, the only detractor being the noise and fumes of vehicles climbing the steep and narrow roads up the face of the escarpment.

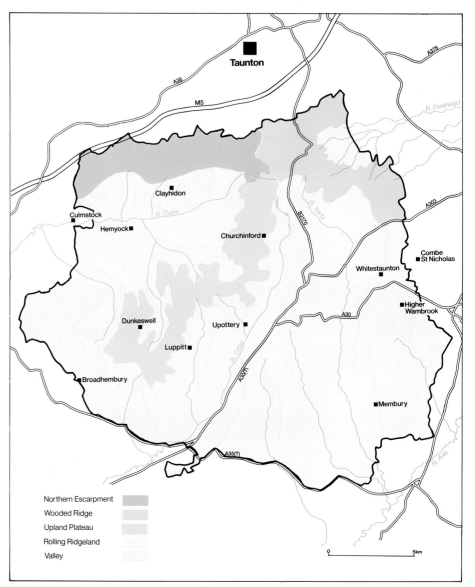

Figure 4. Visual character zones.

The northern escarpment of the Blackdowns is characterised by steep well-wooded slopes.

Long, narrow fingers of ridgeland project out from the main plateaux, and tower above the valleys. Patches of gorse, encircled by deciduous woodland, often occur at the extremity of these ridges.

The gently rolling wooded ridge at the north-eastern corner of the area has magnificent avenues of beech trees along its crest.

The river valleys and combes have steep, wooded upper slopes, small fields of wet, unimproved pasture and lush, overgrown hedgerows.

The northern escarpment

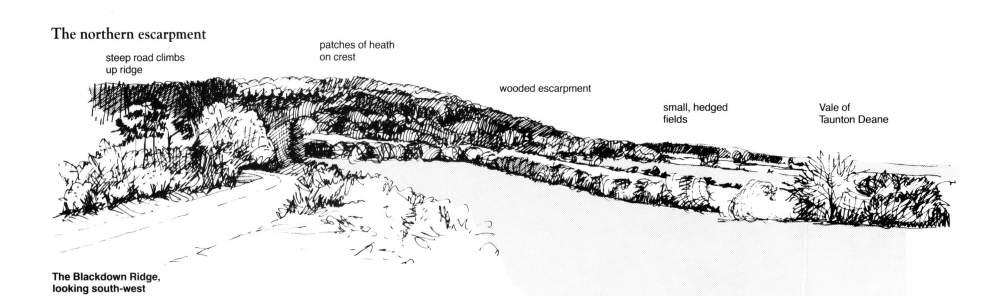

steep road climbs
up ridge

patches of heath
on crest

wooded escarpment

small, hedged
fields

Vale of
Taunton Deane

**The Blackdown Ridge,
looking south-west**

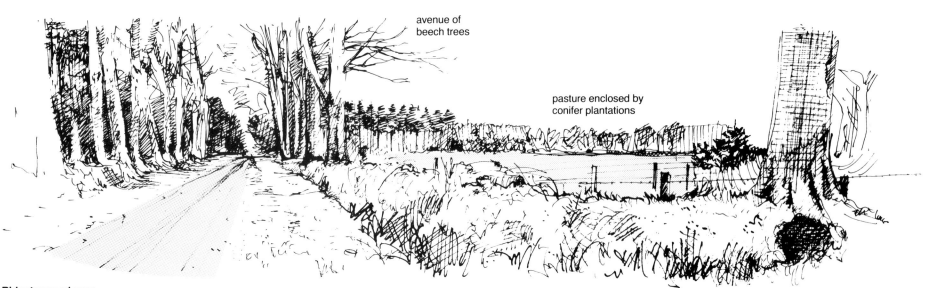

avenue of
beech trees

pasture enclosed by
conifer plantations

**Ridgetop road near
Castle Neroche**

The wooded ridge

To the east of the northern escarpment the topography becomes softer and more rolling, and the northern slopes are cut and folded into an intricate landscape of small hills and incised valleys.

This is a well-wooded area with small secluded fields enclosed by woodland, sometimes deciduous but more often coniferous plantations. Occasionally the pasture is improved and the hedgerows and gates are well maintained, but more typically the farmsteads are small and neglected with rough fields bounded by overgrown hedgerows and scrub, and with wildflowers on the banks.

However, the most distinctive feature is the magnificent beech avenues. Set on mossy banks and spaced at regular intervals these mature trees overhang the main road for some considerable distance, and can also be seen on minor roads and tracks. Some of the fields, too, are edged with beech trees grown on banks, although these have usually been coppiced in the past.

On the northern slopes there are large tracts of coniferous plantation mixed with the deciduous woodland, spilling down to lower slopes of rough, unimproved marshy pasture characterised by overgrown hedgerows and derelict fences. Lower still, there is undulating improved pasture land of expansive fields with fine mature trees, mostly oak, some in the hedgerows but many free-standing in the fields.

The upland plateau

The most obvious feature of the plateau is its roadscape. The very gently undulating land is crossed by long, straight roads, with wide verges to either side edged by low banks topped with hedges of severely clipped beech or occasionally hawthorn. Hedgerow trees are usually mature, isolated, windswept beech or oak.

The hedges curtail views from the road. Views through farm gates tend to be short and wide, a broad sweep of sky over flat fields to a near, hedged horizon. The fields are mainly improved pasture, although there is some arable and also some small blocks of commercial forestry (conifers). Farm buildings are infrequent but prominently surrounded by clusters of large, low-lying, mainly modern agricultural buildings. Where the topography is more rolling there are distant views of similar plateau landscapes, with the edge of the plateau marked by the just visible crowns of trees growing on the steep valley slopes.

In some areas the strong field pattern has been broken and the hedgerows removed to facilitate more extensive farming methods. There is then a sense of bleakness about the longer views across the unbroken stretches of flat plateau. Also interrupting the field pattern, although on a far smaller and more local scale, are road junction improvements, where hedges have been removed to improve sight lines.

In two areas farming on the plateau gives way to other uses. At Trickey Warren in the north there is a forest of radio masts on rough scrubland: a distinctive landmark that detracts somewhat from the surrounding landscape. Also intrusive is the private airfield at Dunkeswell, which features an expanse of tarmac and scattered buildings, including the remains of a World War II airbase. The nearby village of Dunkeswell lies at the head of a valley just off the plateau proper. The village is obviously expanding fast with new housing developments and adjacent land being cleared for industrial units.

The rolling ridgeland

The landscape of the narrow ridges is similar to that of the upland plateau in many respects. Straight roads run along the ridge tops, and the fields of improved pasture are surrounded by wedge-shaped hedgebanks of beech. There are also occasional small blocks of coniferous or mixed woodland. However, the topography is more rolling, the fields are smaller, and there are striking examples of the straight roads being lined with avenues of trees, usually beech or Scots pine.

The roadscape also changes as soon as one leaves the ridgetop roads and heads down into the valleys: the verges disappear, the hedges close in tightly to either side, and as the contours increase the road winds down through the deciduous woodland that typically occupies the steep upper valley slopes.

The narrow topography of the ridges, and their rolling character, mean that there are nearly always views adding variety to the landscape. The near horizon often drops away quite rapidly to reveal tree tops and distant views of other ridges with their wooded slopes.

There are exceptions to the otherwise simple and well-managed farming landscape on nearly every ridge, often at its extremity. These are patches of bracken and gorse encircled by old, deciduous woodland usually occupying a small area of steep-sided high ground. The top of Hackpen Hill is one example; another is Dumpdon Hill in the Otter Valley, which is no longer connected to its ridge. The woods, predominantly oak, are unmanaged and carpeted with primroses in the spring.

The valleys

There are four main valleys in the study area: the Culm, the Otter, the Yarty and the Fivehead. Each exhibits slightly different characteristics, but all share the same basic features of heavily wooded upper slopes, sometimes crowned with moorland, spilling down into a humanised landscape of pasture, hedge and hedgerow trees. There are numerous isolated farmsteads, connected by small, winding roads marked by twisting double hedgerows; and clumps of trees snaking down the valley slopes indicate the presence of combe valleys. Peaceful villages nestle in the flat-bottomed valleys: their church spires are prominent features in the tranquil pastoral setting. From the valley slopes there are extensive views across the field-patterned landscape to distant, wooded ridges.

Different valley topographies add variety. Upstream, and in the incised sections of the rivers, the valleys are V-shaped, and the topography is undulating. Pasture is the dominant land use, and hedges, hedgerow trees, tree clumps and scrub are the most important landscape elements. Downstream, the lower valley sections are broad and open, with flat bottom land but steep sides. Here are found the larger and more prosperous farms, with larger fields incorporating a mixture of arable land and pasture. Occasionally in the lower valleys the impact of development is evident: for example there are views of transmission lines, main roads and urban development outside the area.

The wooded ridge

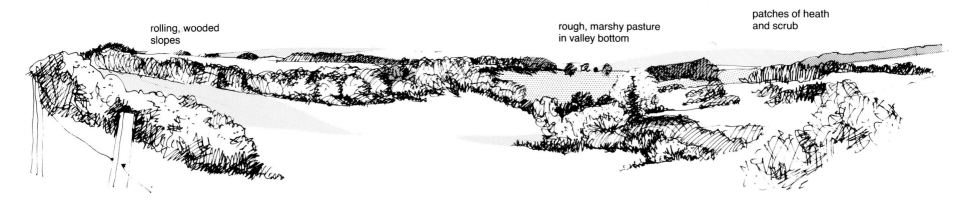

rolling, wooded
slopes

rough, marshy pasture
in valley bottom

patches of heath
and scrub

**View north-west from
near Staple Hill**

The upland plateau

large fields of arable
or improved pasture

wide, straight road
with beech hedges

isolated hedgerow
trees

**Luppit Common,
looking north**

The rolling ridgeland

gorse and bracken on crest of slope, woodland below

views out over patchwork lowland landscape

Looking west from Hackpen Hill

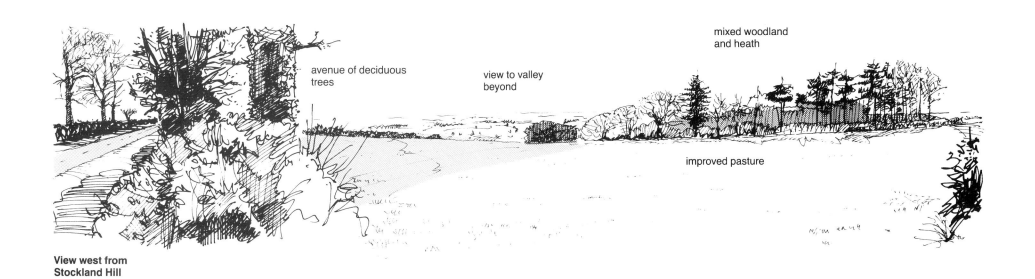

mixed woodland and heath

avenue of deciduous trees

view to valley beyond

improved pasture

View west from Stockland Hill

The valleys

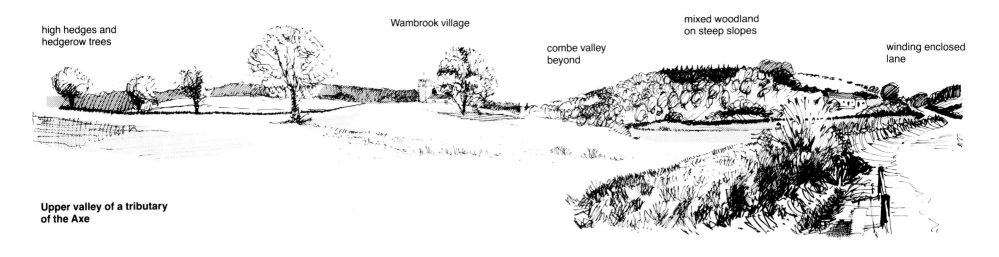

high hedges and
hedgerow trees

Wambrook village

combe valley
beyond

mixed woodland
on steep slopes

winding enclosed
lane

**Upper valley of a tributary
of the Axe**

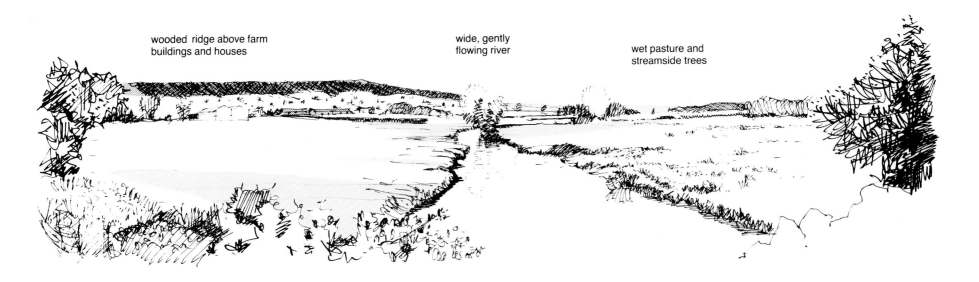

wooded ridge above farm
buildings and houses

wide, gently
flowing river

wet pasture and
streamside trees

The lower Otter Valley

In localised areas several special types of landscape occur

The steep, upper wooded slopes are distinct in themselves. They may consist of coniferous plantations or, more commonly, of unmanaged beech or oak woods with a spring groundcover of wildflowers. Where land has been cleared it is for small, rough fields of unimproved pasture surrounded by well-grown hedges.

Also distinct are the combe valleys. Often enclosed by overhanging trees, these steep-sided valleys contain long, narrow fields of unimproved pasture, sometimes poorly drained, running along the contours. The sense of enclosure is increased by the hedgerows, which are often neglected and overgrown, by the streamside trees, and by the woodland on the upper slopes. Individual stone buildings, backed by trees, nestle in this intricate landscape, often beside a stream, the sound of which is a feature of the combe valley. The occasional farm buildings are usually small and built of timber. These are 'hidden' valleys, suggestive of traditional farming methods, wildflowers and an escape from the pressures of modern day living.

In the lower valley sections, for example in the Culm Valley, water meadows are found. A typical scene is one in which a small river, edged by streamside trees, meanders through lush, unimproved pastures grazed by dairy cattle.

Ecological character

The Blackdown Hills contain a number of semi-natural habitats of ecological interest, including acid heathland, marsh grassland and mire, wet woodland, ancient oak – ash woodland, and ancient hedgerows. The distribution of these habitats is very closely linked to the area's geology and topography, and clearly influenced by its land use history. Some of the habitats — such as the woodlands and hedgerows — are prominent visual features. Others, such as grasslands and mires, are not obvious visually but nonetheless make an important contribution to the area's landscape character at a detailed level, through their mosaic of plant species, colourful scented wildflowers, birdsong and native wildlife.

Acid heathland

Heathland occurs in isolated patches on high ground, on the acidic soils that overly the Greensand. It represents the areas of common land remaining after the parliamentary enclosures. The best example of this type of habitat is the Black Down and Sampford Common area, at the western end of the Blackdown ridge, but throughout the study area other small patches of heathland can be found, typically at the edge of the plateau, above the valley slopes.

The heathland is a diverse community, characterised by gorse, heather and bracken, with birch, rowan and oak scrub. It supports a rich and varied bird life of at least regional importance, which is believed to include nightjars, stonechats, wood larks and golden plovers. In the past, Dartford warblers were also recorded. Several of these species have a limited distribution in Britain.

Marsh grassland and mire

Recent studies [9,10] of grassland and mire communities in the Blackdowns have shown that most of the sites of conservation interest are to be found on the valley slopes, around the Greensand/Keuper Marl or Lower Lias springline, where soils are too wet to be agriculturally improved and are often underlain by peat. These areas are mostly still managed in a traditional way, as hay meadows and rough pasture for cattle.

The main interest is botanical. The majority of sites are only slightly acid, but they have an unusually low calcium content, due to the non-calcareous nature of the Greensand below. This gives rise to distinctive plant communities. A distinguishing feature is the widespread abundance of purple moor grass. In wet areas the vigour of this species is reduced, enabling other species such as heath-spotted orchid, bog asphodel and devil's bit scabious to become established. The wettest areas are characterised by the presence of sphagnum moss and insectivorous plants such as sundews. The species diversity of these grassland and mire sites is often very high.

Wet woodland

Also on the valley slopes, frequently in close proximity to marsh grassland and mire, are areas of wet carr woodland, comprising alder, sometimes with willow or birch. Such habitats are comparatively rare but occur, for example, above Culm Davy and in parts of Prior's Park Wood. They support a varied fauna, including interesting bird species such as the grasshopper warbler, hobby and barn owl. In the vicinity of streams, dippers and kingfishers may also be found.

Ancient oak – ash woodland

Scattered blocks of old semi-natural woodland occur throughout the Blackdown Hills [11,12], with a concentration on the main Blackdown ridge. There is evidence that a high proportion of this woodland has been converted to conifer plantations over the last century. However, ancient broadleaved woodland does survive, for example at Quants, Prior's Park Wood, Adcombe Wood and elsewhere. Much of this woodland was formerly managed on a coppice-with-standards system.

Oak – ash – hazel stands are most common, but in some woods there is a mixture of stand types, including ash – field maple – alder stands, due to local variations in ground conditions. The ground flora is usually dominated by bluebells, but there is also a great display in spring of other flowering species, including lords-and-ladies, wood anemone, wood sorrel, wild strawberry, early dog violet, and common spotted orchid.

The woodlands form a habitat for many invertebrate and vertebrate animal species. Although there are no comprehensive records of species present, they are known to include a range of butterfly species, badgers, and roe and muntjac deer.

Ancient hedgerows

It is evident, both from the area's history of early enclosures, and from observation, that many of the valley hedgerows and banks are very ancient indeed, possibly 600 or more years old. The narrow and winding nature of the lanes, the height of the banks, and above all the great diversity of hedgerow species over comparatively short distances support this claim [7].

The acid, non-calcareous Greensand has given rise to distinctive marsh grassland and mire habitats. These have survived in steep and wet areas that have been managed as hay meadows, in a traditional way.

Black Down and Sampford Common are acid heathland commons that survived the parliamentary enclosures. These and other heathland areas have diverse plant communities and a bird life of regional importance.

Several important semi-natural woodlands, such as Prior's Park Wood (shown here) occur on the Blackdown ridge. These woodlands contain a mosaic of different stand types, and provide a great display of ground flora in spring.

Many of the area's hedgerows may be 600 or more years old. Traditional management, including hedgelaying, keeps them stockproof and helps ensure their survival.

The hedges and banks are an important wildlife habitat. They also display an abundant selection of colourful wildflower species: primroses, red campions, wild orchids, buttercups and many others.

Settlement character

The third strand of the Blackdown Hills' landscape character is their settlement, past and present. How do the area's monuments, historical sites, villages, hamlets and farmsteads affect the landscape today?

Most of the prehistoric activity in the Blackdowns has left few visible signs. However there is evidence that important new archaeological sites may be uncovered in future, for example in the upper Yarty Valley, where there are thought to have been Mesolithic settlements. The later, Iron Age hill forts are a distinctive and well-known feature: Hembury, described as "the grandest earthwork in Devon" [6]; Dumpdon, a familiar landmark on the southern skyline of the hills; Membury, on a ridge north of Axminster; and Neroche, overlooking the Vale of Taunton Deane. All are located on high wooded promontories that still dominate the surrounding landscape, thus reflecting their original defensive purpose. Indeed some of them were later used, together with other nearby hills, as fire beacons at the time of the Spanish Armada.

The valley settlement pattern, together with its fields and hedgerows, is largely a legacy of the medieval period. Fine churches and domestic architecture abound; but there are few castles or large manor houses. In fact, the comparatively poor quality of the land probably meant that few large estates were ever established. Even those large medieval buildings that were built have now mainly fallen into ruin or disrepair. For example, there are only modest visible remains of Dunkeswell Abbey and of the thirteenth century fortified castle of Hemyock. Similarly, there is little physical evidence of the woollen, lace-making, pottery and iron smelting industries that are known to have thrived in the Blackdowns.

From later periods a few key features can be discerned. Stockland Hill provides one of the best examples in Devon of late parliamentary enclosure farms and field systems. Parts of the A303 and A30 represent classic 'turnpike' roads. Wellington Monument, erected in the early nineteenth century, was intended to honour 'The Iron Duke', Sir Arthur Wellesley, who defeated Napoleon at Waterloo and chose Wellington for his title.

But most of all it is the 'ordinary' villages, hamlets and farmsteads of the Blackdown Hills — with buildings of local materials, from a variety of periods — that distinguish the area in architectural terms. Nationally, Devon and Somerset are recognised for the wealth and quality of their rural buildings; in the Blackdowns there seems to be a particular concentration of such buildings. For example, the preliminary findings of the recent resurvey of listed buildings in Devon suggest that a significant number of domestic buildings and churches in the Blackdowns are of outstanding merit (Grade I or Grade II*). Moreover, a very high proportion of farmhouses and cottages are listed Grade II, and the associated farm buildings are also very fine. The traditional appearance of most of the settlements has not been unduly affected by modern development: they retain their quiet rural charm, their historical layout, and their harmonious relationship with the surrounding rural landscape.

Reflecting the geology and the different local traditions of Devon, Somerset and neighbouring Dorset, there is a variety of styles and building materials. Most characteristic are the buildings of flint or chert, dressed with hamstone or brick, and roofed with slate or tile. These predominate in the north and east of the area, and can be seen for example at Whitestaunton and Higher Wambrook. In the south and west the cob and thatch more typical of south Devon is found, for instance at Broadhembury, which is believed to be the most complete sixteenth century village in Devon.

In the Blackdowns there is a particular concentration of high quality rural buildings. Chertstone, dressed with hamstone or brick, is typical of the north and east of the area, for example at Whitestaunton (top left) and Higher Wambrook (above).

To the south and west, cob and thatch are also found, for instance at Broadhembury, which is believed to be the most complete sixteenth century village in Devon (left).

3. Perceptions of the Blackdown Hills through time

Folklore

In folklore, the Blackdown Hills have long had a reputation as being a wild, bleak and forgotten area. The source of the name 'Blackdowns' is not known but it is probably derived either from their 'bleak' or 'black' appearance in winter, or from 'blag-don', meaning 'wolf hill'. In Anglo-Saxon times wolves may well have been found in the Blackdowns, although they subsequently became extinct. In the past, the inhabitants themselves were also perceived as somewhat savage. For example, Matthews, in his *Tales of the Blackdown Borderland* [13], records that:

> "Old folks who knew the hills in the early part of the last century, and knew the people who dwelt there in the one before that, will tell you those parts were very wild and lawless then, and full of smugglers, poachers, coiners and sheep stealers".

The eighteenth and early nineteenth century

The earliest records of how travellers perceived the area date from the beginning of the eighteenth century. At this time the Blackdowns were noted for their views over surrounding enclosed countryside. Many travellers commented on the remarkable views to be seen from the Blackdown ridge, Honiton Hill and Stockland Hill. The views from Hembury and Dumpdon forts were also praised. For example, Celia Fiennes in 1695 said the view from Blackdown was "full of enclosures, good grass and corn", while in 1724 Defoe commented that the view from Honiton Hill "is the most beautiful landscape in the world — a mere picture — and I do not remember the like in any one place in England" [14]. Such views, of wild land tamed by enclosures, were highly valued, but rarely painted because they were thought to be too difficult.

In the picturesque period, which began at the end of the eighteenth century, there is only limited mention of the Blackdowns. The Reverend W. Gilpin was largely responsible for picturesque theory, but in his *Observations on the Western Parts of England* (1798) [15] he fails to mention the Blackdowns although he says of the Axe and its tributaries, which include the Yarty, that: "if any vallies (sic) can be said to laugh and sing, these certainly may".

The local picturesque traveller was the Reverend John Swete, whose twenty volumes of notes and watercolours are in the Devon Record Office. He visited the Blackdowns in 1794 and 1801. Apart from noting that the villages were "mean and thatched", he restricted his interest to the ruins of Dunkeswell Abbey, and to the panoramic views. However Murray in his *Handbook for Travellers in Devon and Cornwall* (1856) [16] gave more attention to the Blackdowns. He visited Hemyock church and castle and Dunkeswell Abbey, and praised the view from the hills of the secluded valleys. He also had praise for the Otter Valley at Honiton, which he described as "a valley remarkable for its graceful lines and rich culture, and bordered by detached eminences pleasingly grouped".

The reasons for the Blackdowns' modest popularity at this time are fairly easy to adduce. They did not have the features that appealed. Romantic scenery had very deep, heavily wooded valleys, with fast rivers and majestic ruins; rustic villages and cottages were not of interest; nor were flat-topped hills and plateau areas.

The late nineteenth century

In the late nineteenth century wild scenery became more popular. Moors, marshes, fens and fells came into fashion, and in paintings often formed the backdrop to heroic human activity. Dartmoor and Exmoor in particular were the source of much artistic inspiration, but the Blackdowns rather less so, perhaps because by this time their landscape had begun to change. With the late parliamentary enclosures it had been at least partially tamed.

A number of literary sources give impressions of how the Blackdowns were seen at that time. R. D. Blackmore, although more commonly associated with North Devon through *Lorna Doone*, was raised in Culmstock on the edge of the Blackdowns, and his novel *Perlycross* is set partly in Culmstock and Hemyock. Snell describes the setting for *Perlycross* in *The Blackmore Country* [17]:

> "The Blackdowns, generally, have been enclosed and turned into farms; and although one sometimes stumbles on desolate fields with patches of gorse, mindful of their ancient savagery, this does not affect, to any appreciable extent, the character of the country. On the whole, a ride or walk across the long level chines is not specially delightsome, save indeed for the wholesome air and an occasional glimpse of a fairy-like 'mappa mundi' spread out at their base. It is only when one decends into charming little villages, like Hemyock or Dunkeswell, or Broadhembury, with their orchards fair and hollyhocks, that complete satisfaction is attained and then it is attained".

Yet an element of wildness remained. In 1863 the Blackdowns Mission was established. The purpose of this Seventh Day Adventist mission, based at Clayhidon and lead by one George Brealey, was to bring the gospel to the poor inhabitants of the remote and sparsely populated areas. Although there had been a long tradition of non-conformism in the Blackdowns, dating from the late seventeenth century onwards, when George Brealey arrived parts of the Blackdowns were still thought to be wild and godless:

> "the major part of the people could neither read nor write.....in some of these districts there existed as gross ignorance and superstition as are to be found in many so-called heathen lands" [18].

The view from the hills north of Honiton, much praised by Defoe, can still be seen today, and is probably little changed.

Rustic, pastoral landscapes — including cottages, villages, farmyards and gardens — rose to favour around the turn of the century. From then on, landscapes such as the Cotswolds, Dorset Downs and Blackdowns became more popular.

Field patterns like these were a source of inspiration to the Camden Town Group of artists early this century, and have inspired many others since.

Dec 10 1794.

Dunkerswell Abbey

View from Panchey Down looking down upon Blackborough Church, Beacon Hill (with the firs on it) and Lord Egremont's House (on the extreme right.) Coloured on the spot Sept.r 12. 1804.

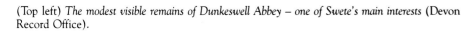

Mode of Trimming Whel-stones for Scythes on the Whel-stone Hills, Panchey Down, and one of the entrances into the side of the hill. This passage entered 300 yards horizontally. Sketched Sept. 12. 1804.

HACKPEN HILL AND CAMP, FROM UFFCULME.
Coloured on the spot, April 3. 1049.

(Top left) *The modest visible remains of Dunkeswell Abbey – one of Swete's main interests (Devon Record Office).*

(Top right and bottom) *Hutchinson watercolours illustrating popular pastoral scenes (Devon Record Office).*

The early twentieth century

In the twentieth century two general trends in landscape appreciation have influenced the popularity of the Blackdown Hills. One, stemming from abstract art, is the love of the formal, structural, geometric qualities in some landscapes. The other is the love of vernacular, rustic landscapes, specifically villages, cottages, orchards and farms.

The former tradition almost appears to have started in the Blackdowns, although perhaps largely by coincidence. Robert Bevan, a professional artist of private means, studied with Gaugin at the turn of the century, and was impressed by Cubism in Paris. Returning to his home at Applehayes near Clayhidon he began to paint landscape views from the tops looking over the fields, concentrating on the geometric pattern caused by the field boundaries and the different crop colours. These seem to be the earliest paintings in England that take the pattern of the countryside as the chief subject. The result was far reaching and subsequently such patterns have been sought throughout Britain by many artists.

Moreover, Applehayes became the weekend retreat for a considerable circle of painters, mainly those associated with the now-popular Camden Town Group. They included Spencer Gore and Charles Ginner, who are known to have painted in the Blackdowns; and possibly also Harold Gilman and W. R. Sickert.

HUNT'S PATH

ON THE BLACKDOWN RIDGE

During this period, love of the rustic and vernacular spread to many parts of England, largely from Sussex and the Weald. Areas such as the Cotswolds, the Dorset Downs, and the Blackdowns began for the first time to be favoured, for this reason. Pastoral scenes were painted, usually of villages, cottages or farmyards. Membury and Broadhembury are two villages in the area that were regularly depicted in paintings and drawings.

Literature and guidebooks of the early twentieth century also demonstrate the rising popularity of the Blackdown Hills, and there are some charming guidebook descriptions from this period. In 1927, Donald Maxwell, in his *Unknown Somerset* [19] wrote of the Blackdowns:

"Happy is the country that has no history, and happier still is the country-side that has no popular attractions. Beyond the monument to the Iron Duke, an obelisk that stands upon the heights above Wellington, there is nothing about the Blackdown Hills of such an obvious nature that scores of thousands of people in chars-a-bancs must flock to see it. Consequently you may roam about, even in the middle of holiday August, and find lanes almost deserted and shady glades of woodland without even picnics, and come upon little farms and secluded homesteads nestling under the long ridge — a ridge that is dark with pine or bright with mountain ash".

Landscape views typical of the Camden Town Group. Spencer Gore's *Applehayes* (1909), Collection Ulster Museum (left); R. P. Bevan's *Near Hemyock, Devon* (1918), Whitworth Art Gallery, University of Manchester (top left) and *A Devonshire Valley* (1918), Royal Albert Memorial Museum, Exeter (above).

A few years later Maxwell Fraser wrote:

> "their villages are as unselfconscious as they are lovely in their rural simplicity.... the hills are quiet and serene.... a real haven of refuge for those in search of healing peace.... Apart from their remoteness from the bustle of modern life, the charm of these hills lies in their woods and the wonderful views across the fair counties of Somerset and Devon. Not even the Quantocks are more thickly wooded than the Blackdowns...." [20].

The value of the Blackdowns landscape was formally recognised probably for the first time in 1932, when the Devon Branch of the Council for the Protection of Rural England commissioned the architect and planner, W. Harding Thompson, to prepare a survey of Devon [21], with suggestions for its 'preservation'. This survey identified 'areas of special landscape value', which "contain features of such outstanding character that their preservation as open space is most desirable". Extensive areas of the Blackdowns were labelled as areas of special landscape value.

Perceptions of the Blackdowns today

In the last 50 years, perceptions of the Blackdowns have not changed markedly. They are still little known compared with other scenic areas. This can be ascribed to two factors. First, the Blackdowns remain, to this day, an area that is remote and relatively inaccessible. They are bypassed to the north by the M5, and only one major trunk road, the A30/A303, passes through. Many of the by-roads are winding, single-track and poorly signposted: they do not attract a multitude of tourists. The second factor is the location of the hills, straddling the Somerset/Devon border, and not identified closely with either county.

The fact that the Blackdowns are still comparatively little known is also evident in the dearth of modern guidebooks. There is only one recent guidebook about the Blackdowns as such [22]. This focusses mainly on the area's history and draws attention to a number of well-known historic figures linked with the Blackdowns.

Perhaps the best-known figure is the Duke of Monmouth, illegitimate son of Charles II, who in 1685 led a Protestant rebellion against his father's Catholic successor, James II. He marched through the Blackdowns, on his way to Taunton and ultimately to defeat at the Battle of Sedgemoor. Many of his supporters are said to have come from the Blackdowns. Another famous figure was Henry Addington, the first Viscount of Sidmouth, who was raised at Upottery Manor and subsequently became Prime Minister in 1801-4. The Duke of Wellington is also associated with the Blackdowns, because of the monument, although in fact he had little to do with the area directly. At Wolford, south of Dunkeswell, lived the Simcoe family. John Graves Simcoe, who came from Wolford and retired there, was the First Lieutenant Governor of Upper Canada (Ontario). He was also directly responsible for the enclosure of some 5,000 hectares of land in the Blackdowns early last century. Wolford Chapel, owned by the Ontario Government, is a memorial to him.

A more recent figure is the eldest Kennedy brother, Joseph, who was killed in operations from Dunkeswell airfield during World War II.

However, modern perceptions of the Blackdown Hills are probably best derived directly from the opinions of those who know the area well. In the course of preparing this report we met a wide range of local residents and others who know the Blackdowns, and invited their views about its landscape character and value.

A commonly expressed view was that the Blackdowns represent a "lost world" of remote valleys and wide open spaces. They offer a "place to escape to", to "step back in time", to see "England as it was". They are old-fashioned, unspoilt, unknown, bypassed, peaceful and quiet. There was a wide measure of agreement as to these qualities. Features that were specifically mentioned as being distinctive and valuable were the escarpment, ridges, knobs and forts; the fine field patterns, conserved intact; the diversity of vegetation, especially the wildflowers; and the buildings, barns, churches and villages.

Overall, there seemed to be a broad consensus that the Blackdowns is a valuable landscape, which should be conserved, and indeed the Blackdowns Association, a local group with over 200 members, has been formed specifically for this purpose.

4. Landscape change

As the purpose of the AONB designation is to conserve the natural beauty of the landscape, it is important to have an appreciation of how the landscape has changed in the recent past, and how it may change in future. Are these changes likely to threaten its landscape character and qualities?

Landscape change this century

There is little or no documentary evidence about recent landscape change in the Blackdown Hills as such. Analysis of historical Ordnance Survey maps and air photographs would no doubt yield such evidence, but only a cursory examination of these sources has been possible as part of this study. The following information, gleaned mainly from secondary sources, suggests how the landscape may have changed since 1900.

In common with Somerset and Devon as a whole, it appears that there has been a swing from mixed farming, including cereals and roots, to grass and livestock rearing, particularly dairying. This has been accompanied by grassland improvement, and the making of silage rather than hay.

A look at the 1931-37 Land Utilisation Survey map shows extensive areas of heath, moorland, commons and rough pasture along the main Blackdown ridge, between Black Down Common and Staple Hill. Many of these areas have now disappeared, suggesting their continued conversion to improved grassland. Such change is still going on, for example to the west of Trickey Warren, where areas of wet heath and scrub have recently been converted to pasture.

Change in the character of the Blackdowns grassland is also evident from the Somerset Trust for Nature Conservation's report on the grassland resource of the Blackdown Hills [9]. This estimates that less than 2 per cent of the grasslands in the area are now of conservation value: a decline of more than 95 per cent over the last fifty years. Mire habitats, too, have been lost.

The total area of woodland in the Blackdowns has probably changed very little [23], but its character has changed. During the 1950s and 1960s particularly, many broadleaved woodlands were converted to coniferous woodland. Although this trend seems to have slowed, some coniferous afforestation is still taking place and has caused local controversy. The scale of the broadleaved woodland loss is probably considerable: reports by the Nature Conservancy Council [11,12] estimate that in the period 1930 to 1986, Somerset and Devon respectively lost 43 per cent and 40 per cent of their ancient broadleaved woodlands that are more than two hectares in size.

There has also been consolidation of agricultural holdings and field amalgamation, with resultant loss of hedgerows and hedgerow trees. It is impossible to estimate the extent of this change, but it is likely to have occurred mainly on the plateau and in the valley bottoms. For example, Brimley Hill and the lower Culm Valley are known to have lost a significant number of hedges and hedgerow trees in recent years.

Modern building and development has been quite limited, with a few notable exceptions. These are the radio masts at Trickey Warren, Dunkeswell Airport, new housing and industrial development at Dunkeswell, an electricity transmission line across the southern part of the area, a number of large new agricultural buildings, and the expansion of the village of Hemyock to include a milk processing plant. Elsewhere the only new development has been modest additions to existing housing stock.

Forces for future landscape change

No one can say with any certainty how the landscape will change in future, but the most likely forces for change can be identified.

Despite current moves towards more extensive and diversified agriculture, it is possible that in the Blackdowns agricultural intensification may continue. This is especially likely if the current proposal to grant the Blackdowns less favoured area status succeeds. This status carries with it improved headage payments for livestock, and higher rates of grant for capital works such as land drainage and pasture reseeding. These improvements in turn could lead to further losses of grassland and mire habitats as well as hedgerows.

There may also be continued pressures for afforestation, as farmers are encouraged to plant trees through the Woodland Grant Scheme. Provided broadleaved trees are planted, this is not necessarily a threat, but care will need to be taken to avoid the loss of ancient field patterns and other valued ecological habitats such as the remaining heaths and commons.

The future of existing hedgerow trees, avenue plantings and broadleaved woodlands is by no means assured. Many of these plantings date from early last century. They are now mature or overmature and often in urgent need of replanting or management to facilitate regeneration. Without appropriate action, they may be lost.

Built development, too, may bring changes. Already significant changes have occurred, particularly due to the housing development at Dunkeswell, which was granted planning permission prior to local government reorganisation. The current development plans make no provision for additional new housing on a large scale. However, there is no doubt that the Blackdowns are, and will continue to be, a popular place to live and to visit. Pressure is likely to come, increasingly, in the form of proposals for housing and tourism developments. These may include proposals to convert redundant farm buildings (often of high architectural quality) to dwellings and second homes, develop new services and tourist attractions, and improve the area's road network.

Finally, major mineral development is unlikely, although not impossible. In the past there have been proposals to extract silica sand from two areas, but these have been refused.

A threat to landscape quality?

Compared with many other areas of the countryside the Blackdown Hills have experienced only limited landscape change over the last century. Nor are they subject to major immediate development threats, but rather to gradual, cumulative changes. Their landscape is the product of interactions between natural and human influences over many centuries; there can and should be no question of 'fossilising' it in its present form. On the other hand there is a need to be aware of what the 'key' qualities of the landscape are and in what ways they are vulnerable to change.

These issues are examined in the final chapter.

Mature hedgerow trees, avenue plantings and broadleaved woodlands are frequently in urgent need of replanting or management.

Coniferous afforestation, particularly during the 1950s and 1960s, has changed the character of the woodlands of the Blackdown Hills.

New built development — such as this housing at Dunkeswell — has had an adverse landscape impact in some areas, and increased tourism in future may bring new pressures.

31

5. The importance of the Blackdown Hills landscape

The importance of a landscape is hard to measure. It depends upon a multitude of factors, not least of which is personal preference. Nonetheless, it is now widely accepted that it is possible to give a reliable assessment of landscape value on the basis of "informed opinion, the trained eye, and common sense" [3]. This approach was recommended by the Inspector at the public inquiry into the North Pennines AONB designation in 1985, and has since been formally adopted by the Countryside Commission. It is an approach that we have used in the preparation of this report.

The purpose of this chapter is to identify and highlight the outstanding qualities of the Blackdown Hills landscape. This is necessary not only to explain why the designation is being made, but also to assist the local authorities who, according to Countryside Commission policy on AONBs [4], will have the major responsibility for implementing the designation. Their first task will be to prepare a Statement of Intent, setting out future policies for the Blackdown Hills landscape.

Outstanding qualities

In our view it is quite clear, both from the nature of the landscape itself, and from the opinions of those who know the area well, that the landscape of the Blackdown Hills is outstanding. It is outstanding because it has a subtle combination of unusual, even unique characteristics. These make it a distinctive landscape, with its own special identity; an identity that artists, writers, local residents and visitors — as well as the consultants — strongly feel should be conserved. There are at least four ways in which the landscape is outstanding.

An isolated and unspoilt rural area

The Blackdowns are particularly important for their unspoilt rural character. There are now few parts of England where such an extensive area of countryside is so untouched by the pressures of modern development. Even tourism pressures, which have now made their mark in most of our attractive rural areas, including many AONBs, have largely bypassed the Blackdowns. In their winding lanes, hidden valleys and traditional villages there is a keen sense of stepping back in time; of release from the stresses of everyday living; of the links between nature and humanity. Society today places a high value on these qualities. Aesthetically, also, there is a strong appreciation of the rustic, vernacular, pastoral landscapes with which the Blackdowns are so well endowed.

Because the area has been relatively undisturbed by development, ancient landscape features, special habitats, archaeological and historical remains have survived intact where elsewhere they would have been destroyed. Further study and research are needed to bring to light the full extent of the area's conservation interest, but already it is evident that it is considerable.

The twisting, double hedgerows that snake down valley sides.

Distinctive and outstanding features of the Blackdown Hills landscape include Iron Age hill forts and Armada beacons (Culmstock Beacon); the visual pattern of heathland, wooded slopes and valley pasture; and the unspoilt villages with their wealth and variety of rural architecture.

A unique geology

The geology of the Blackdowns (together with that of the adjoining East Devon AONB) is unique in Britain, and is one of the area's strongest unifying features. Although most people visiting the Blackdowns are unaware of the geology as such, its influence on landscape character is very evident. It has given rise to the distinctive topography of flat-topped plateaux, sharp ridges, and spring-lined valleys. The springs in turn have created the characteristic pattern of rough grassland, mire and wet woodland vegetation on the valley sides. The non-calcareous nature of the Greensand has meant that these plant communities are particularly diverse. Moreover, the geology has provided a native building material, the chertstone, which is quite uncommon.

There is nothing quite the same elsewhere in Britain, because nowhere else is there the same geology. Although Upper Greensand is found in a narrow band at the foot of the North Downs in Surrey, its composition there is different, and the area is heavily developed. On the Haldon Hills, south of Exeter, a small outcrop of Upper Greensand also occurs. This area, although once attractive, is now marred by major road developments.

A diversity of landscape patterns and pictures

The visual quality of the landscape is very high, and can be best expressed as 'patterns and pictures'. Although the scenery is immensely varied, on travelling through it one is very conscious of particular images that are repeated again and again. There are the beacons, knobs and monuments, which tower above the valleys; the long views over field-patterned landscapes, which have inspired so many artists; the enclosed, twisting lanes; the steep slopes with their ancient woodlands; the patches of heath and common, bog and mire; and the parliamentary enclosures with their fine avenues of beech and Scots pine. All these features are of special value.

At a more detailed level there is also an infinite variety of visual and ecological interest: in the heathland bird life, the diverse mosaic of wetland and woodland ground flora, and the colourful wildflowers on the hedges and banks.

A landscape with architectural appeal

The overall landscape pattern is punctuated by a wealth of small villages, hamlets and isolated farmsteads of considerable architectural value. Although Devon and Somerset are recognised nationally for their fine rural architecture, here in the Blackdowns there is a special concentration of such architecture, and its vernacular character is remarkably well preserved.

Its charm lies in the way the buildings fit so naturally into their surroundings; in their age, which is predominantly fourteenth to seventeenth century; in their use of chert, as well as cob and thatch; and in the fascinating mixture of building styles and traditions. Located mainly in the valleys and reached only by narrow winding lanes, little traffic or recent development mars the appeal of these settlements and buildings, and in summer their beauty is enhanced by bright cottage gardens.

Vulnerability to change

Together these qualities make the Blackdown Hills a very special place. The area is under no immediate threat of landscape change but nonetheless there are some trends that, if allowed to become established, could lead to fundamental alterations in the appearance of outstanding scenic features.

In our view, the following changes, in particular, could have a significant adverse effect on the scenic features of the Blackdowns:

- further reclamation and 'improvement' of heathland, scrub, grassland and mire habitats;
- coniferous afforestation;
- the loss of distinctive avenue and hedgerow trees;
- the removal of hedgerows, especially where it affects the ancient field patterns of the combes and valleys;
- any large-scale housing or other built development;
- road widening or realignment schemes.

These changes, in turn, suggest a number of conservation issues that are likely to arise in future. Among the issues that will need to be addressed are:

- how to retain heathland, grassland and mire habitats and encourage their traditional management as hay meadows and rough pasture;
- how to discourage further conifer planting and direct new broadleaved planting away from important ecological habitats and ancient field patterns;
- how to ensure appropriate management and regeneration of broadleaved woodlands, and replacement of mature avenue plantings and hedgerow trees;
- how to retain the ancient hedges of the combes and valleys, and conserve their wildflower and wildlife interest;
- how to accommodate new development into the villages and hamlets without damaging their traditional architectural character;
- how to deal with the increasing tourism pressures that seem likely to occur.

Conclusion

In summary then, the Blackdown Hills is of outstanding importance as perhaps the archetypal English rural landscape. Its geology, topography and history of medieval and parliamentary enclosures have clearly influenced the development of the landscape. It has quite distinct visual, ecological and architectural characteristics. In the past it has been valued mainly as a vantage point for panoramas over the surrounding countryside, but in the twentieth century its field patterns and scenes of rustic life have generated new aesthetic interest. Its outstanding landscape qualities are its isolated and unspoilt character; its unique geology; its diversity of the landscape 'patterns and pictures'; and its architectural appeal.

In the words of Donald Maxwell [19] it is a:

"thoroughly English piece of country...quite unspoilt by any mass admiration and exploitation and quite unconscious of being picturesque".

Some of the beauty of this area results from the ancient deciduous woodland, and the majestic avenues of trees that dominate the ridge tops.

6. References

(1) National Parks Committee, *Report of the National Parks Committee (England and Wales)*, HMSO, 1947.

(2) Wildlife and Countryside Act 1981 Section 53(2), HMSO, 1981.

(3) Countryside Commission, *Landscape assessment: a Countryside Commission approach*, CCD 18, Countryside Commission, 1987.

(4) Countryside Commission, *Areas of outstanding natural beauty: a policy statement*, CCP 157, Countryside Commission, 1983.

(5) Edmonds, A E et al, *British regional geology: South-West England*, HMSO, 1969.

(6) Hoskins, W G, *Devon*, David and Charles, 1972.

(7) Rackham, O, *The history of the countryside*, Dent, 1986.

(8) Hoskins, W G, *The making of the English landscape*, Penguin, 1970.

(9) Somerset Trust for Nature Conservation, *The grassland resource of the Blackdown Hills*, unpublished report to the Nature Conservancy Council, 1987.

(10) Pulteney, C, 'Mire Vegetation of the Blackdown Hills', *Nature in Somerset*, 1988, pp 10 – 12.

(11) Nature Conservancy Council, *Somerset inventory of ancient woodland (provisional)*, unpublished report, 1986.

(12) Nature Conservancy Council, *Devon inventory of ancient woodland (provisional)*, unpublished report, 1986.

(13) Matthews, F W, *Tales of the Blackdown borderland, The Somerset folk series no 13*, Somerset Folk Press, 1923.

(14) Chope, R P (ed), *Early tours in Devon and Cornwall*, David and Charles, 1967.

(15) Gilpin, W, *Observations on the western parts of England relative chiefly to picturesque beauty*, 1798.

(16) Murray, *A handbook for travellers in Devon and Cornwall*, 1856.

(17) Snell, F J, *The Blackmore country*, Adam and Charles Black, 1911.

(18) Brearley, W J B, *'Always abounding' or Recollections of the life and labours of the late George Brealey, evangelist of the Blackdown Hills*, John F Shaw, 1889.

(19) Maxwell, D, *Unknown Somerset*, Bodley Head, 1927.

(20) Fraser, M, *Somerset*, Great Western Railway Company, 1934.

(21) Thompson, W H, *Devon: a survey of its coast, moor and rivers with some suggestions for their preservation*, University of London Press, 1932.

(22) Webber, R, *The Devon and Somerset Blackdowns*, Robert Hale, 1976.

(23) Devon County Council and Nature Conservancy Council, *The changing face of Devon, Exeter and Taunton*, Devon County Council and Nature Conservancy Council, 1979.

CW00686952

The Cotswold landscape

A landscape assessment
of an area of outstanding natural beauty,
prepared for the Countryside Commission
by Cobham Resource Consultants

Countryside
COMMISSION

Published by:
Countryside Commission
John Dower House
Crescent Place
Cheltenham GL50 3RA
© Countryside Commission 1990

Distributed by:
Countryside Commission Publications
19/23 Albert Road
Manchester M19 2EQ
CCP294
Price £6.50

Contents

British Library Cataloguing in Publication Data

The Cotswold Landscape: a landscape assessment. – (CCP: 294)
1. England. Cotswold. Landscape
I. Cobham Resource Consultants. II. Great Britain.
Countryside Commission
719.09424
ISBN 0–86170–249–2

Figures

Acknowledgements

Thanks are due to all the various organisations and individuals who helped us in the preparation of the report. Their local knowledge and constructive comments proved to be invaluable.

The study team comprised: Julie Martin, Miranda Plowden, David Nicholson, Peter Howard and Peter Hamilton.

We are grateful to the following for illustrative material: Peter Hamilton; Countryside Section, County Planning Department, Gloucestershire County Council; Paul Felix; Cheltenham Art Gallery and Museums, Gloucestershire; Bridgeman Art Library; M S Fripp; John Gere; Southampton City Art Gallery; The Manchester City Art Gallery; Martin Brown; British Waterways.

Cover photo: *The Cotswold scarp near Wotton-under-Edge.*

Designed and produced by The Edge – Cheltenham

Foreword

The Cotswolds Area of Outstanding Natural Beauty (AONB) was designated by the National Parks Commission in 1966. It is the second largest AONB in England and Wales, stretching from just north of Bath to Chipping Campden in Gloucestershire.

The Countryside Commission has now conducted a review of the boundaries of the AONB. The impetus for the review came from the Secretary of State for the Environment in 1982, when he made a statement following the Commission's review of its policy towards AONBs. While the concept of AONB designation was supported in the statement, the Commission was asked both to re-examine the remainder of its programme of new designations and to review the boundaries of the existing designated areas.

The Cotswolds were considered a priority for review because it was widely recognised that there were large areas of outstanding landscape adjacent to the designated area, particularly at the northern and southern extremities. The Commission also considered that in parts of the existing area, the landscape has been materially changed by agricultural practices and as a result of development, and no longer met national standards.

As part of its submission to the Secretary of State for the Environment the Commission asked Cobham Resource Consultants, as independent landscape consultants, to prepare an assessment of the landscape character and quality of the Cotswolds, including the major extensions proposed. It is intended that the assessment should provide a context for the Commission's proposals, particularly for the major changes.

While the views expressed are those of the consultants, the Commission believes that they make an important contribution to the understanding of the landscape of the modified area, which the Commission considers to be of national importance.

Sir Derek Barber
Chairman
Countryside Commission

Preface

In preparing our assessment, we – Cobham Resource Consultants – have asked ourselves two questions about the meaning of the AONB designation and how these relate to the Cotswolds.

Firstly, what does 'natural beauty' consist of? We have been guided by the definition of natural beauty given in the Wildlife and Countryside Act 1981 [1] and by the Countryside Commission's own interpretation of natural beauty [2]. We conclude that, although the emphasis should be on visual quality, geology, topography, flora and fauna, historical and cultural aspects are also relevant.

Secondly, and perhaps more importantly, in what way must an AONB be outstanding? The answer – according to Countryside Commission AONB policy [3] – is that it should be of such fine landscape quality that there is national as well as local interest in its conservation. This implies that it should have features that are not only distinctive, but also unusual or even unique. It suggests that these features should be highly valued, not just by landscape specialists but also by the general public, among whom there should be a broad consensus as to the area's importance and beauty.

These considerations have guided us in the preparation of the landscape assessment, for which we have adopted the approach recommended by the Countryside Commission in its document *Landscape assessment: A Countryside Commission approach* [2].

We begin by describing the area factually, in terms of its physical features and history, and its visual, ecological and architectural character. Next, we examine how the Cotswolds have been perceived through time, by writers and artists, visitors and local residents. We also consider how the landscape is changing, and how it may change in the future. Finally, we spell out as clearly and simply as possible the area's essential landscape qualities, based on common sense, objective perception and our own professional judgement.

1. The development of the Cotswold landscape

Introduction

The Cotswold Hills represent the best known section of the outcrop of oolitic limestone that stretches right across England, from Lyme Bay on the Channel coast to the North Sea between Filey and Redcar. The most dramatic scenery occurs on the north-west face of the Cotswolds, which forms a prominent escarpment overlooking the wide plains of the Vales of Berkeley, Gloucester and Evesham. Here, beechwoods and historic villages shelter under the edge, within its bays and combes; and there are spectacular road descents. In places the escarpment is deeply incised, providing a magnificent setting for towns such as Bath and Stroud. To the south-east the land dips away gently as a plateau, with rolling wolds and river valleys. Broad, open views of arable fields and woodland alternate with more intimate scenes of village, pasture and water meadow. Throughout the area, local stone is the principal building material, and the villages blend subtly with their surroundings.

Perhaps more than any other English landscape, that of the Cotswolds reflects the physical and human influences that have moulded it through time. These influences have created an immensely varied landscape, but one which nonetheless has many common features and a clear identity.

Physical influences

The geology of the Cotswolds (Figure 1) has had a very important impact upon the landscape. Rocks of the Jurassic period predominate [4]. The strata dip gently towards the south and east, and at the south-eastern extremities of the area are found the youngest rocks: small pockets of Oxford Clay and Cornbrash (a coarse, crumbly limestone).

Beneath these, and covering much of the AONB, is the Great Oolite, a limestone much prized as a building stone. To the south, between Bath and Stroud, the Great Oolite forms the Cotswold scarp. However, to the north the Great Oolite has been eroded from the face, exposing the underlying Inferior Oolite. It, too, is good building stone.

The colour of the oolites varies from silvery white to golden ochre, depending on the iron oxide content of the rock. There is a tendency for the Inferior Oolites to contain more iron, and hence have a brighter colour, than the Great Oolites.

Around the northern and western edges of the area the Lias shales, sandstones and siltstones of the Lower Jurassic are exposed on the scarp face and valley sides. These rocks are softer and weather more easily than the limestone above. As a result, slides and slips have occurred on the face, giving rise in many areas to a hummocky appearance. The Lias also forms the floor to the low-lying marshy Vale of Moreton, which projects southwards into the northern end of the Cotswolds' massif.

Topographically, too, the Cotswolds are complex (Figure 2). The general dip to the south-east is confused by a series of east – west fault lines, and by some folding in the west. The escarpment, which in places reaches more than 300 metres in height, has progressively eroded south-eastwards as a result of fluvial and periglacial processes over thousands of years. The retreat has followed lines of weakness, and this has resulted in the creation of deep, wide valleys around Bath, Stroud and, to a lesser extent, Winchcombe. At the same time, a number of outlying hills such as Bredon Hill and Oxenton Hill have survived as remnants of a former scarp face that lay further to the west. At the northern extremity of the hills the scarp face is stepped back, behind the Vale of Moreton. Here the face is less pronounced, and extends as a long finger of high ground to Edge Hill in Warwickshire. On the dip slope, shallow valleys break up the smooth undulating expanses of the dip slope plateau.

The drainage of the Cotswolds is closely linked to their geology. The differential permeability of the oolites and the underlying Lias gives rise to springs at the junction of these two rock series, particularly on the scarp slope. On the dip slope, streams are reduced in length and volume over the permeable limestone beds due to underground seepage, and many stretches of stream flow as winterbourne, reflecting higher winter water tables. Rivers on the scarp slope are generally short, the exceptions being the Avon and Frome, which appear to have cut through the scarp slope and captured the headwaters of rivers that may once have flowed east. On the dip slope there is a series of important streams, including the Evenlode, Windrush, Leach, Coln and Churn. All of these are tributaries of the Thames.

Many of the Cotswold soils are derived directly from the bedrock and are therefore alkaline in nature. Other soils are formed from alluvial deposits and also some scattered glacial deposits. Thin, well-aerated brashy soils derived from limestone are typical of the steeper slopes and are particularly common on the western escarpment. They tend to be red-brown in colour, and their calcium carbonate content may have been reduced by leaching processes. These soils are typically very dry and thus are good for sheep grazing and arable farming. In the valley bottoms and in some places on the dip slope, deeper alluvial and more clay-rich soils are found, which are less well-drained and therefore more commonly used for cattle grazing. There is little high quality agricultural land: grades 3 and 4 are typical of most of the area.

Human influences

Human influences on the Cotswold landscape are great and go a long way towards explaining the landscape patterns that can be perceived today.

The earliest settlers in the area arrived in Mesolithic times, about 6000–5000 BC [5]. The evidence for this shows in the form of Mesolithic flint implements that have been discovered scattered in modern day arable fields at many sites in the Cotswolds. At this time, the landscape of the area was probably covered by woodland, dominated by lime [6]. Small-scale forest clearances were made by Mesolithic tribes, but clearance on a large scale did not take place until Neolithic times, 4500–2000 BC.

Fig 1 LOCATION MAP

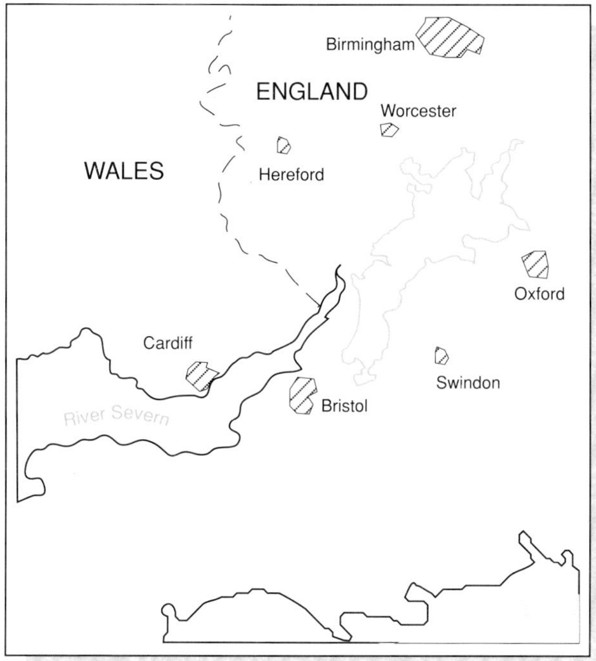
Birmingham
ENGLAND
Worcester
WALES
Hereford
Oxford
Cardiff
Swindon
Bristol
River Severn

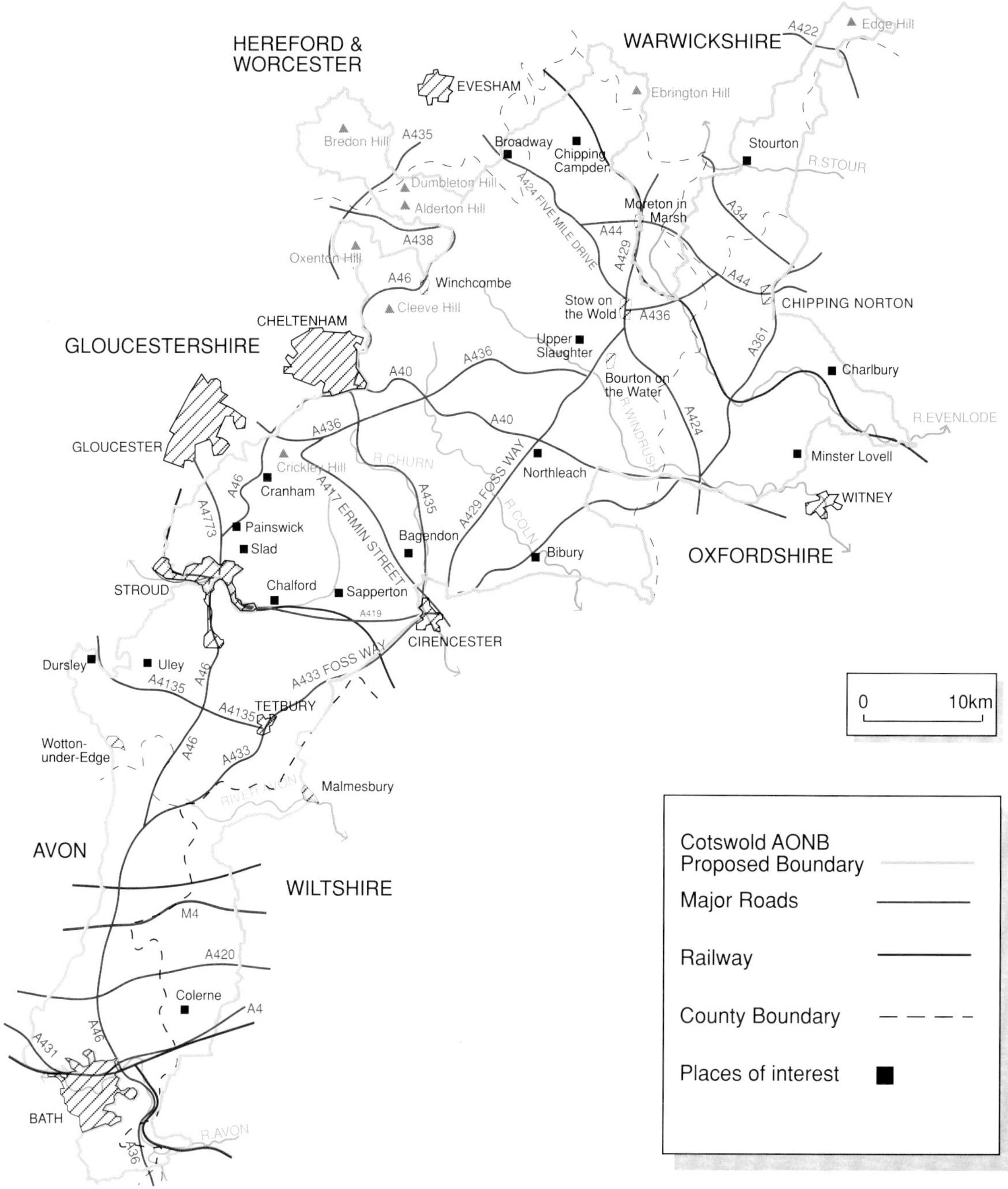
HEREFORD &
WORCESTER
WARWICKSHIRE
A422
Edge Hill
EVESHAM
Ebrington Hill
Bredon Hill
A435
Broadway
Chipping Campden
Stourton
R.STOUR
Dumbleton Hill
Alderton Hill
Moreton in Marsh
A34
A44
A438
A424 FIVE MILE DRIVE
A429
Oxenton Hill
A46
Winchcombe
A44
CHIPPING NORTON
Cleeve Hill
Stow on the Wold
A436
CHELTENHAM
GLOUCESTERSHIRE
Upper Slaughter
A361
A436
A40
Charlbury
Bourton on the Water
R.WINDRUSH
A424
R.EVENLODE
A40
GLOUCESTER
A436
Crickley Hill
R.CHURN
Northleach
Minster Lovell
A46
Cranham
A417 ERMIN STREET
A435
A429 FOSS WAY
WITNEY
A4173
Painswick
R.COLN
Slad
Bagendon
Bibury
OXFORDSHIRE
STROUD
Chalford
Sapperton
A419
CIRENCESTER
Dursley
Uley
A4135
A46
A433 FOSS WAY
A4135
TETBURY
Wotton-under-Edge
A46
A433
Malmesbury
AVON
WILTSHIRE
M4
A420
Colerne
A4
A46
A431
BATH
A36
R.AVON
0
10km
Cotswold AONB Proposed Boundary
Major Roads
Railway
County Boundary
Places of interest

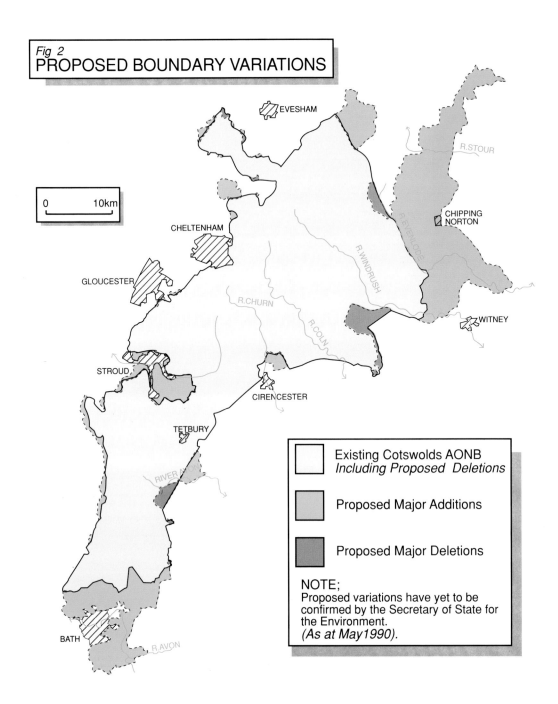

Fig 2
PROPOSED BOUNDARY VARIATIONS

EVESHAM

0   10km

R.STOUR

CHELTENHAM

CHIPPING
NORTON

GLOUCESTER

R.WINDRUSH

R.EVENLODE

R.CHURN

R.COLN

WITNEY

STROUD

CIRENCESTER

TETBURY

RIVER

Existing Cotswolds AONB
Including Proposed Deletions

Proposed Major Additions

Proposed Major Deletions

NOTE;
Proposed variations have yet to be
confirmed by the Secretary of State for
the Environment.
(As at May 1990).

BATH

R.AVON

The main visible remains from this period are long barrows and chambered tombs, such as Hetty Pegler's Tump, near Uley, and Belas Knap, south of Winchcombe.

During the Bronze Age, from 2000 BC, the culture of the Beaker Folk was characterised by worship at stone circles or henges; the Rollright Stones near Chipping Norton are a relic of this period. In the Iron Age which followed, from 750 BC, tribes organised into larger and more cohesive groups. This enabled the construction of large earthen forts on sites of strategic advantage. Many such Iron Age hill forts can still be seen in the Cotswolds today; indeed, at least seventeen are found along the escarpment alone. Bredon Hill Fort and Meon Hill Fort in the northern Cotswolds are among the most impressive examples. During the Iron Age, Bagendon, north of Cirencester, is believed to have been a tribal capital. Iron Age people were probably also responsible for the prehistoric ridgeways – green tracks that today still follow the hill crests, on light soils. Best known of these is the Jurassic Ridgeway, which follows the oolites right across England.

The Romans left an important impression on the landscape of the Cotswolds. Like earlier cultures, they preferred to settle on light and easily cultivable soils; hence, the remains of villas and other settlements have been found throughout the area, although a more lasting influence on the landscape is that of the Roman roads. The Foss Way spans the full length of the Cotswolds, connecting Bath to Leicester, representing the limits of Roman settlement in the first century AD. Today, as the A429, it links Cirencester to several of the Cotswolds' main towns, including Bourton-on-the-Water, Stow-on-the-Wold and Moreton-in-Marsh. Other influential Roman roads include Ermin Street (now the A417 from Cirencester to Gloucester); Akeman Street (a Roman route from Cirencester to St Albans); and Ryknild Street, which leads north from the Foss Way towards Birmingham.

It seems likely that the Saxon period saw the main settlement of the region. The Cotswold plateau was almost certainly settled before the heavily wooded valleys. Hill-top villages, in particular, are suggestive of great antiquity and may have been occupied continuously from Roman times or earlier. The presence of water was a most important factor in the siting of settlements; hence, many villages are found along the springline on both scarp and dip slopes. The principal land use was sheep grazing and the extensive sheep walks, still so typical of the Cotswold landscape, were established during this period. Thus, in the view of W G Hoskins, "the landscape of the Cotswold uplands ... was even in Saxon times much as we know it today" [7].

By the time of the Domesday Survey in 1086 most of the present-day villages were already in existence; because the land was not productive, the settlement pattern was one of large villages rather than of scattered farmsteads. The Survey shows that large areas were under agriculture, mainly as part of extensive ecclesiastic and feudal demesnes, with sheep grazing, and arable crops using an open field system. The only substantial wooded areas that survived at this time were a belt of woodland along the escarpment edge; the woodlands west of Cirencester, which formed a Royal Forest; and the wildwood of Wychwood Forest, near Charlbury.

In parts of the Cotswolds, prehistoric and historic remains, including tumuli, earthworks and hill forts, form visible landscape features such as at Belas Knap.

Straight Roman roads, such as the Foss Way, are also distinctive features.

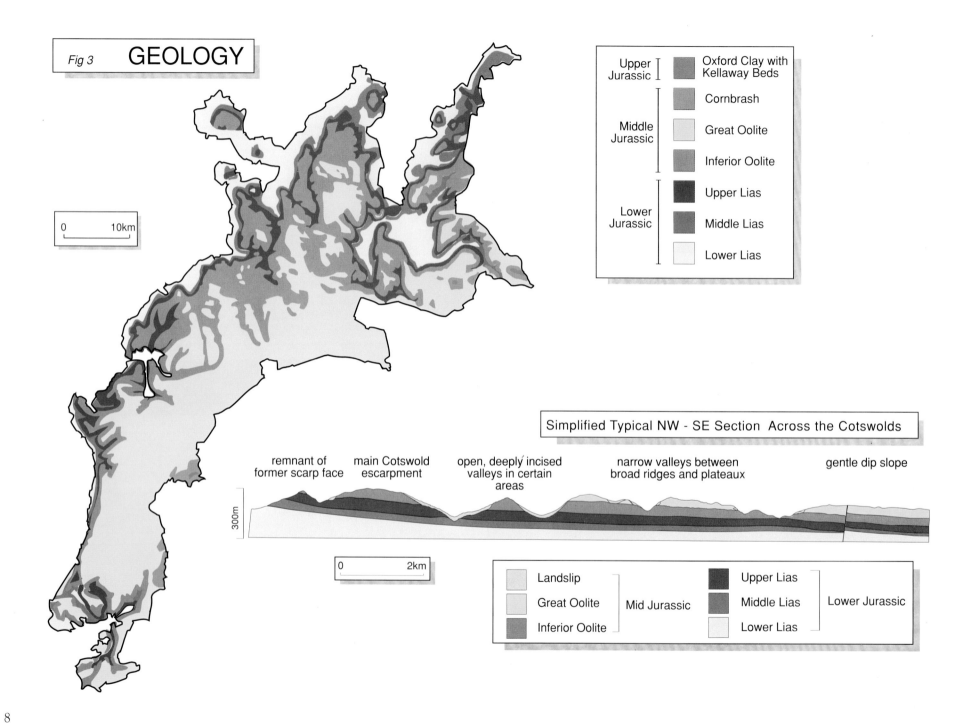

Fig 3 **GEOLOGY**

0   10km

Upper Jurassic — Oxford Clay with Kellaway Beds

Middle Jurassic — Cornbrash

Great Oolite

Inferior Oolite

Lower Jurassic — Upper Lias

Middle Lias

Lower Lias

Simplified Typical NW - SE Section Across the Cotswolds

remnant of former scarp face | main Cotswold escarpment | open, deeply incised valleys in certain areas | narrow valleys between broad ridges and plateaux | gentle dip slope

300m

0   2km

Landslip

Great Oolite — Mid Jurassic

Inferior Oolite

Upper Lias

Middle Lias — Lower Jurassic

Lower Lias

8

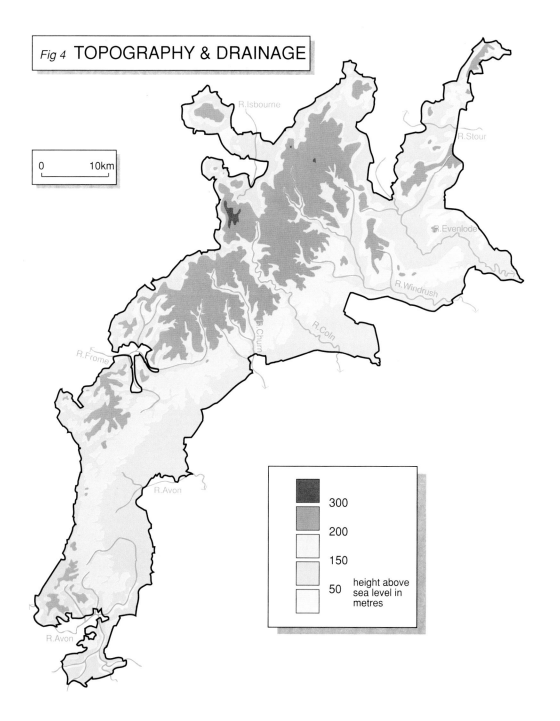

Fig 4 TOPOGRAPHY & DRAINAGE

0   10km

R.Isbourne

R.Stour

R.Evenlode

R.Windrush

R.Coln

R.Churn

R.Frome

R.Avon

R.Avon

300

200

150

50 height above
sea level in
metres

During the centuries that followed, most landholdings remained in the control of the church and lay lords, many of whom were based outside the area. For example, the Abbots of Gloucester, Evesham and Westminster all held manors in the Cotswolds. Local owners included the Cistercians of Hailes Abbey, the Carthusians of Hinton Priory and the Lords Berkeley of Beverston. During the fourteenth and fifteenth centuries, and especially after the Black Death, the lords consolidated their demesnes and created large pastures enclosed by stone walls. Transhumance, the seasonal movement of stock from low to high ground, was practised.

The late Middle Ages was perhaps the most formative period in the history of the Cotswolds, for during this time its villages took on their present character. Thanks to good grazing and the many small streams that provided water for washing and fulling, a prosperous wool trade developed. Small market towns grew up, including Painswick, Northleach and Chipping Campden. Stately Gothic churches were built in the Perpendicular style, together with fine gabled merchants' town houses, and numerous more modest dwellings. All of the buildings were constructed of the local oolites, which formed not only walls but also window mullions, chimneys and roofs.

Following the dissolution of the monasteries the monastic lands were granted to Tudor knights and courtiers. Many fine country houses and parks were established during the succeeding centuries, including Compton Wynyates, Sherborne Park, Dyrham Park, Badminton and Cirencester Park, and a wide range of architectural styles is represented in the great houses of the Cotswolds, ranging from Tudor to Georgian. Outside the parkland the enclosures continued, although on the high ground of the wolds little new enclosure took place until the parliamentary enclosures of the late eighteenth and early nineteenth centuries. A mixture of stone walls and hedgerows was used; avenues, shelterbelts and plantations were added, and turnpike roads were built.

In parallel with these rural changes the towns developed and grew, particularly along the scarp face in the southern Cotswolds. The cloth industry, by this time dead in much of the north and east Cotswolds, expanded during the seventeenth, eighteenth and nineteenth centuries in the valleys around Dursley, Stroud, Chalford and Painswick. The industry was founded upon local water power and deposits of Fuller's Earth, which were used for cleansing and felting the woollen fabric. Originally a cottage industry, by 1800 cloth-making had so expanded that large multi-storey stone buildings were erected to house the looms. Unpretentious terraced houses were built along the hillsides, while the mill-owners erected Georgian and Palladian town houses. However, by 1850 the industry was in decline, partly due to competition from the new steam-powered mills of the north. Thus the Cotswolds escaped the worst aspects of industrialisation, and few further landscape changes were made during the Victorian period.

These, then have been the main influences on the development of the Cotswold landscape. There have been modest changes during the course of the last century (see Chapter 4) but the basic physical and human influences are still clearly evident. The next chapter examines the character of the landscape today.

Medieval villages in the Cotswold vernacular occur throughout the area. Bledington in the Evenlode Valley is one of the many dozens of villages with conservation area status and numerous listed buildings.

St Mary's Mill, Chalford, is an example of eighteenth century development within the Cotswold landscape.

2. The character of the landscape today

In analysing the character of the Cotswold Hills today, it is helpful to consider the landscape from several different perspectives. Primarily, we have looked on the area as a visual resource, and thus its visual character is described in some detail. However, we are also conscious that it is an ecological resource, and that its ecological characteristics may not be immediately obvious to the casual observer. These too, therefore, are discussed. Finally, we look at the landscape as human habitat, and consider the character of its settlements. Together these three separate 'strands' make up the character of the landscape as a whole.

Visual character

In visual terms the Cotswolds can be divided into a number of different zones of broadly similar character (Figure 6):

● the dramatic edge landscape of the main escarpment face;
● the incised landscapes around Bath, Stroud and Winchcombe;
● the outlying hills to the north and west of the escarpment;
● the broad area of high wold that lies behind the escarpment in the northern Cotswolds;

● the finger of lower wold country that extends from Chipping Norton to Edge Hill;
● the dip slope landscape found all along the south-eastern edge of the Cotswolds;
● the ridges and valleys east of Bath and Stroud, which are transitional between the incised landscapes and the flatter, rolling landscapes of the dip slope.

Figure 5 illustrates the way in which these character zones relate to geology and topography.

The edge landscape

The edge landscape of the Cotswolds has a major visual impact when seen from the Vales of Berkeley, Gloucester and Evesham, below. The escarpment that creates the 'edge' runs south-west to north-east and is dramatically steep in places. The highest point is Cleeve Hill near Cheltenham, more than 300 metres high. The scarp is irregular and hummocky; although generally straight, it also has bays and inlets.

Over most of its length the scarp is clearly defined, and quite distinct from the plain below. The face is well-vegetated, with dense beech woodlands, clumps of trees, isolated trees, hedgerows and scattered scrub. Scrub in particular is more characteristic of the edge landscape than of other types of landscape. Fields vary in

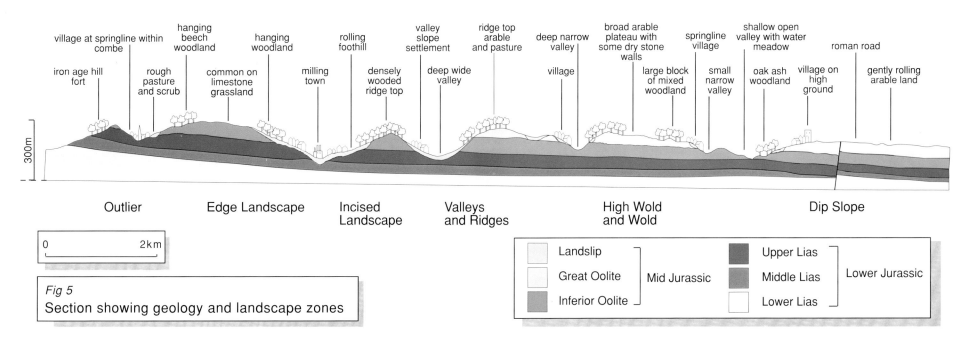

Fig 5
Section showing geology and landscape zones

Landslip
Great Oolite   Mid Jurassic
Inferior Oolite

Upper Lias
Middle Lias   Lower Jurassic
Lower Lias

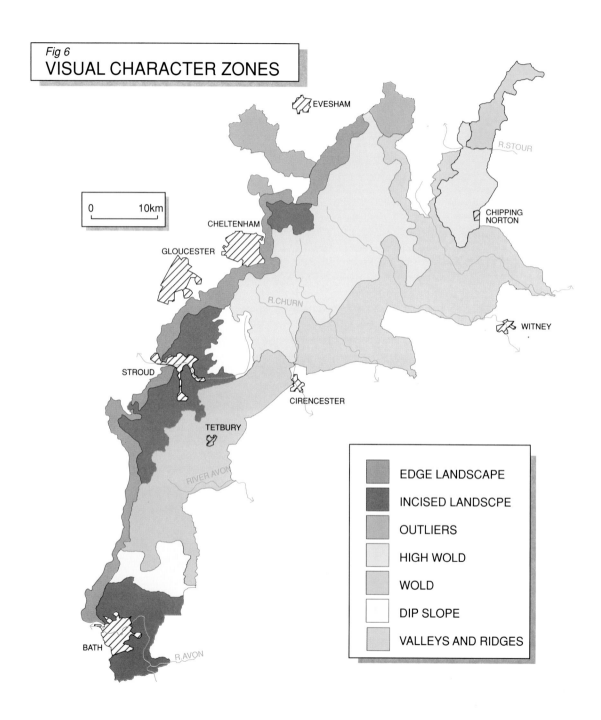

VISUAL CHARACTER ZONES

Fig 6

0   10km

EVESHAM

R.STOUR

CHIPPING NORTON

CHELTENHAM

GLOUCESTER

R.CHURN

WITNEY

STROUD

CIRENCESTER

TETBURY

RIVER AVON

BATH

R.AVON

	EDGE LANDSCAPE
	INCISED LANDSCPE
	OUTLIERS
	HIGH WOLD
	WOLD
	DIP SLOPE
	VALLEYS AND RIDGES

The edge landscape; scarp face from near Wotton-under-Edge.

size and the principal land use is grazing, by both cattle and sheep, on rough pasture and meadow. On the top of the escarpment, commons, such as Cleeve Common, are a distinctive feature.

Settlement on the scarp face itself is rare, apart from isolated farmsteads that nestle among woodland, within valleys and combes. However, at the hill foot (the springline) is a series of attractive small towns and villages, some of which have the very apt suffix 'Subedge'. Roads are either aligned along the flat plain at the scarp foot or climb the scarp face along river valleys. On the hill crest there are many fine viewpoints and landmarks, including Broadway Tower, and numerous Iron Age hill forts. In the south, where the escarpment is lower and less marked, these landscape patterns are less clear-cut.

The edge landscape; view south-west from Cleeve Hill over the Vale of Gloucester.

The incised landscape

Incised landscapes are found in three distinct areas around Bath, Stroud and Winchcombe, where valleys and ridges radiate outwards from the towns sited on the main valley floor. The area around Bath includes the main Avon and Limpley Stoke Valley, as well as important side valleys such as that of Wellow Brook. Near Stroud, the incised landscape extends north to Painswick, east to Chalford, and southwards to include a series of valleys known as the Bottoms. South of Winchcombe, the valley of the Isbourne also forms an incised landscape.

The landform is characterised by deep, wide valleys. Viewed from below the valley spurs interlock, with undulating ridges above and rolling foothills below. The latter are particularly prominent where villages are sited within depressions of the rolling topography, among scattered trees and a woodland backdrop.

The incised landscape; Golden Valley at Chalford.

The deep valleys are accentuated by densely wooded ridge tops that often dominate the skyline and distant horizons. Typically trees snake down the valley slopes, becoming clumps and more scattered around the foothills. Otherwise-hidden watercourses are easily picked out by winding fingers of woodland. Most of the tree cover consists of mature deciduous specimens, with very little evidence of commercial or shelterbelt planting. Occasional irregular hillslopes that have not been utilised for grazing have been allowed to develop a covering of scrub. This feature is sometimes associated with localised cultural landscapes, such as long barrows and hill forts.

Mature hedgerow field-boundaries consisting of dense thicket vegetation are found in the valleys, where the small fields relate intimately with the landform and the dominant land use is pasture. Arable farming in larger field units is found on the broader ridge tops, where drystone walls are a common field boundary. Although in the valley bottoms there are factories and mills, the complex makeup of the landscape is such that they become accessories in the wider panorama rather than focal points.

13

The escarpment formed by the oolites is the most prominent topographic feature of the Cotswolds. The scarp face is dramatic and varied, with hills and combes.

Painswick is situated in a typical incised landscape – deep and wide, with valley slope woodlands.

The edge landscape is characterised by its steep escarpment, with fine panoramic views over the wide plain below.

In the 'Golden Valley' above Stroud, villages and hamlets line the wooded hillside, and there are small mills and factories surviving from the eighteenth century cloth industry.

Dumbleton Hill, one of the Cotswold outliers, is a relic of an ancient escarpment that lay further north-west.

The high wold is a large-scale, open landscape with large blocks of woodland and arable land.

Bredon Hill, the largest Cotswold outlier, has an outward-facing radial form, and neat, regular fields.

The wold landscape is similar to the high wold, but smaller scale. This is partly because in this area much of the oolite has been eroded away, and the surface geology is predominantly Lias.

The incised landscape; view towards Painswick from Scottsquar Hill.

Settlements within the incised landscapes are typically nucleated, located in the valley bottoms or in niches up the valley sides. Often, hamlets are strung out along the slopes, linking the main centres. Chalford, in the 'Golden Valley' above Stroud, is a particularly beautiful example of a hillslope settlement, where the houses line the hill in terraces overlooking the River Frome in the gorge below. It is unusual to find isolated farmholdings or properties on the plateau above, although there are occasional exceptions, including a number of large estates and historical buildings that overlook foothill settlements. Settlements are small, with individual properties huddled close together; church spires and towers associated with the villages often feature prominently in the landscape. The roadscape is normally tortuous and complex. Narrow lanes passing through arch-shaped tree overhangs, past cottages clinging to the terraced slopes, are especially delightful.

The very varied relationships between landform, vegetation, land use and settlement in this zone create scenery that is at the same time dramatic, intimate and humanised.

The outliers

Five hills in the north of the AONB – Oxenton Hill, Bredon Hill, Alderton Hill, Dumbleton Hill and Ebrington Hill – comprise the outliers. Their landscape character is determined largely by their topography – physically and visually discrete from the surrounding landscape. Indeed, each is a true geological outlier, a relic of an ancient escarpment that lay further north-west than the existing edge.

The most distinctive feature of the outliers is their outward-facing radial form, in that watercourses and field boundaries appear to radiate from the central high point. This pattern contrasts visually with the inward-facing 'star' shape of the incised valleys. Like the main escarpment, several of the outliers are crowned by hill forts, woodlands and scrub, from below which they often present a smooth, polished dome shape, with neat, regular fields, mainly of rough pasture.

The high wold and wold

In the northern part of the Cotswolds, to the east of the edge and incised landscapes, the topography becomes softer, the valleys smaller and narrower, and there are broad plateau tops. This is the undulating landscape of the high wold. On the plateau tops it is a large-scale, generally open landscape, characterised by large blocks of woodland and arable land; but tucked away in the valleys are lush, intimate pastoral and village scenes. The sense of contrast between the two is marked.

The principal types of vegetation are occasional wooded ridges, clumps of trees and sporadic skyline trees. Fingers of trees line the watercourses giving additional variety to the landscape. Well-treed hedgerows are the typical field boundary in the valleys, but drystone walls and post-and-wire fencing predominate on the plateau

The outliers; Dumbleton Hill from the north.

Dip slope; view over the Lower Evenlode Valley.

tops. Woodlands, plantations and shelterbelts are important landscape elements; although usually small scale, in certain localised areas they may be extensive. For example, the area north of Cirencester is heavily wooded; and several large woodlands occur in the west, near the scarp face. Estate parkland is also an important feature, found throughout the high wold, perhaps especially on the edge of the Vale of Moreton.

Villages are generally found along the spring line and are nucleated, sometimes centred around features such as commons and greens. On higher ground, there are tiny hamlets and isolated farmsteads. Extensive areas are unspoilt, but there are other areas in which developments such as farm buildings, radio masts, pylons and airfields, cause varying degrees of visual intrusion.

The components of the wold landscape, which occurs in the area from Stourton north to Edge Hill, are similar in every way to those of the high wold, but on a smaller scale. The wold is physically lower and less wild and open. The plateau areas are less prominent, and the rolling hills between the small valleys often permit views into hollows in the landscape which appear tucked away and unspoilt.

The dip slope

South and east of the wolds the topography becomes yet more gentle and open and there is a gradual transition to a dip slope landscape, which covers a large area along the eastern side of the Cotswolds. Here the hills are not the dominant feature of the landscape, but line the horizon as grey or soft blue distances, according to prevailing skies.

As in the wolds, the plateau is dissected by rivers such as the Windrush and Coln, but the valleys are much broader because they are further downstream. In some cases the valleys are so broad as to give the impression that they are simply undulations in the plateau. Small, narrow valleys occur occasionally, but are typically very shallow.

The plateau is flat and open, the impression one of a very large-scale landscape that is simple and smooth in texture. The dominant land use is arable farming. Large arable fields are separated by neat hedgerows or post-and-wire fencing. Drystone walls occur, but are less common than on the plateaux of the wolds. The Roman roadscape of the Cotswolds is particularly noticeable here: major roads are broad and straight and sited on high ground. In the marshy valley bottoms, for example near Minster Lovell, are wetland trees (poplars, willows and alders) and grazed water meadows, which in spring are sprinkled with wild flowers and inhabited by coots, moorhens, herons and warblers.

The valleys and ridges; nr Colerne north-east of Bath.

Arable farming is a dominant land use on the dip slope.

Especially characteristic of the dip slope are the marshy valley bottoms and water meadows, for example along the River Coln.

The dip landscape is yet more gentle and open than the high wold and wold, as seen in this view of the broad Evenlode Valley.

Beech woodlands are found along much of the escarpment. The national importance of such woodlands for nature conservation is widely recognised.

Tucked away within the high wold landscape are small, narrow valleys with lush, intimate pastoral and village scenes, as shown in this view of Upper Slaughter.

The valley and ridge landscapes found north-east of Bath and Stroud, are characterised by narrow but deeply incised valleys with broad, flat intervening ridges.

The wold;
Mine Hill.

For the most part, the area is sparsely wooded, tree cover being mainly in the form of isolated copses and hedgerow trees. However, there are some densely wooded areas, often associated with large estates and parks such as Westonbirt, Cirencester Park, Cornbury Park and Wychwood Forest. These may influence the scenery well beyond their boundaries.

Dip slope settlements are usually located on high ground above the rivers, or on the flatter valley slopes. They are larger and often more spread out than the villages of the wolds, and isolated farmsteads are more common. The building style is similar to other Cotswold villages, but there has been more recent development and 'suburbanisation'. The dip slope landscape is also adversely affected in some areas by large new farm buildings and young coniferous plantations.

The valleys and ridges

Finally, there is a landscape type which is a pleasing combination of both incised and dip landscapes. It occurs to the north-east of Bath, and east of Stroud, and is characterised by narrow but deeply incised valleys with broad flat intervening ridges.

The valley bottoms and slopes contain very similar components to those of the incised landscapes, such as rolling foothills, pastureland broken by thicket hedges, settlements huddled together in topographic depressions, and winding sunken roads. However, the valley features tend to be on a smaller scale, and more intimate. By contrast, the ridge tops are very wide, and have similar characteristics to the dip landscape, with elements such as open mixed arable and pastoral farming, stone walls, wide straight roads and spreading suburbanised settlements.

Overall, this landscape is small scale and diverse, with a texture that varies from rough in the valleys to smooth on the ridges. It differs from the high wold landscape (which also has many of the characteristics of the incised and dip landscapes) in that the contrast between the valleys and ridges is even more marked. In the high wold the valleys and plateaux form a 'whole', with all elements of the topography in the

The high wold, the Coln Valley;
nr Compton Abdale

20

Beech woodland is a prominent visual feature. Its distribution is closely linked to the area's geology and topography.

Unimproved limestone grassland is an important semi-natural habitat which is now increasingly scarce, both regionally and nationally. It survives in parts of the Cotswolds, for example at Cleeve Common.

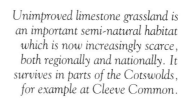

Commons may also include areas of scrub habitat. Scrub occurs, for instance, on Minchinhampton Common, shown here.

Steep roofs of limestone slates, stone window mullions, rectangular dripstones and four-centered arches over the doorways are key features of Cotswold vernacular architecture.

Cotswold rivers such as the Evenlode support a wide range of aquatic plants and animals and attractive marginal vegetation.

harmony. In the valley and ridge zone, there is almost a sense of two very separate and different landscapes in juxtaposition.

Ecological character

The Cotswolds contain a number of semi-natural habitats of ecological interest, including primary beech woodlands; other ancient woodlands; unimproved limestone grasslands; scrub; and streams and marshes [8]. The distribution of these habitats is very closely linked to the area's geology and topography, and clearly influenced by its land use history.

The natural vegetation of the Cotswolds is thought to have consisted of dense mixed woodland. From earliest times, the woodland clearances resulted in the development of areas of thorn scrub and grassland, while woodland survived on the less accessible slopes, valleys and clay lands. The areas of greatest ecological interest today are those that contain remnants of these ancient vegetation types.

Some of the habitats – particularly the woodlands – are prominent visual features. Others, such as the limestone grasslands, are less obvious visually but nonetheless make an important contribution to landscape character at a detailed level through their patterned plant communities, wild flowers, butterflies and birdsong.

Beech woodlands

The Cotswolds' escarpment, especially between Birdlip and Dursley, supports extensive tracts of primary beech woodland which appears to be the climax vegetation on the thin calcareous soils. The national importance of these woodlands for nature conservation is widely recognised. They lie almost entirely on the Inferior Oolite and strongly resemble the 'beech-hangers' of the south-eastern chalk downs. Forest management, coupled with the dense shade cast by beech, has led to the dominance of this species almost to the exclusion of others. Nonetheless, there is often a rich ground flora which may include rarities such as helleborines, alpine woundwort, birds-nest orchid and common wintergreen. In landscape terms, the very 'emptiness' of the woods caused by the dearth of shrubs, combined with the grace of the trunks and canopy, gives them great simplicity and beauty.

Other ancient woodlands

Other ancient woodlands of various types are also found in the Cotswolds. On the clay soils of Fuller's Earth and landslip areas are occasional examples of woods, where ash is the dominant tree species. In the southern part of the Cotswolds, for example at Colerne Park in Wiltshire, wych elm woodlands occur; and there is a single example, at Boxwell, of a very rare woodland type dominated by box.

Elsewhere, in the wolds and on the dip slope, the ancient woods contain a mix of species [9]; both high forest areas with species such as oak, ash, maple and cherry, and coppice with standards, are found. Typically these woodlands are located on the upper slopes of valleys and on the flat plateau tops where there are deeper soils. The best and most extensive examples are Oakley Wood (part of Cirencester Park), Withington and Chedworth Woods, Guiting Wood and Wychwood. Canopies are more open than in the beech woodlands and this allows the establishment of a very diverse understorey, including species such as wayfaring tree, dogwood, spindle, privet, hazel, brambles and wild roses. A wide variety of ground flora species is found, including wood anemone, yellow archangel, Solomon's seal, meadow saffron and many others. The range of fungi, butterflies, birds and other animals is also considerable and includes mammals such as foxes, badgers and fallow deer.

Unimproved limestone grassland

Another important semi-natural habitat of the Cotswolds is unimproved grassland, which is now increasingly scarce both locally and nationally. In the Cotswolds the majority of such grassland occurs on the calcareous soils of the Jurassic limestone. It is found particularly on steep, uncultivated ground, typically on the scarp face, and in the dry valleys or 'bottoms' of the dip slope. In many areas it relies for its continued existence on traditional management such as communal rough grazing – for example at Cranham Common and Cleeve Common.

These grasslands support a very diverse flora of calcicole (lime-loving species), which provides in turn an excellent habitat for butterflies such as the marbled white, the blue butterflies and the fritillaries. Many unusual grasshoppers and other insect species occur. Locally uncommon breeding birds include wheatear and stonechat.

Scrub

In the management of grasslands it is often important to control the growth and invasion of scrub. However, some scrub areas may form valued habitats in their own right, representing the transition zone between grassland and woodland.

Scrub habitats in the Cotswolds commonly include such species as hawthorn, dogwood and wayfaring tree. They may provide habitats for butterfly species and cover for a large number of birds, including uncommon long-eared owls. Bredon Hill is a fine example of Cotswold scrub and limestone grassland.

Streams and marshes

Cotswold rivers such as the Windrush and Evenlode support a wide range of aquatic plant and animal life. Marginal marsh vegetation, unimproved meadows and alder/willow carr enhance their interest; while flowering plants such as marsh marigold, yellow flag and occasionally marsh orchid lend colour. Mayflies and caddis flies, trout and other fish species, as well as herons, reed warblers, grey wagtails and dippers, are found where the watercourses are undisturbed and unpolluted. Otters are sighted occasionally.

Settlement character

The last but by no means the least important strand of the Cotswolds' landscape character is its long history of settlement, and particularly the architectural character of their villages and small towns.

Archaeological and historical features

Much of the Cotswolds has been settled since prehistoric times, and this is reflected in the large number of archaeological sites and monuments in the area. Many of these, such as Crickley Hill, are multi-period sites.

The early phases of settlement – Neolithic, Bronze Age and Iron Age – have left comparatively few visible signs, except for modest tumuli (sometimes emphasised as landscape features by nineteenth century planting) and the Iron Age hill forts of the scarp and outliers. The Roman legacy, in the form of villas and the main road network, is observable but not prominent. The Saxons were responsible for choosing the sites of most of the Cotswolds' villages, for early church building, and for the creation of the distinctive sheep walks of the wolds, which were subsequently enclosed by medieval landlords. Other medieval landscape features that survive in certain areas are ridge and furrow; fish ponds; deserted medieval villages like that near Moreton-in-Marsh; and forestry banks such as the 'park pale' that encloses Oakley Wood. From the sixteenth century onwards the large private landowners of the Cotswolds transformed woodland to parkland; built fine country houses; and carried out further enclosures.

Villages and towns

It was the late medieval craftsman builders, working for both rich merchants and burghers, who made the single most important contribution to the Cotswold landscape as we see it today. Their work was characterised by the use of stone from local quarries, so that entire villages were built from the same material. A distinctive style was established which became the archetype for the whole of the limestone belt [10], and which has been copied by subsequent generations of builders through to the present day. The architectural importance of the Cotswold idiom is recognised today in the area's huge number of listed buildings and conservation areas.

The best building stone of the northern Cotswolds came from the triangular area between Stroud, Burford and Chipping Campden. Here the oolite is comparatively soft when first extracted, and therefore is easily cut and dressed. This quality gave rise to a fine traditional craftsmanship, which flourished from the late fourteenth century to the middle of the eighteenth century, financed by the prosperous wool trade. Further south the somewhat harder Bath stone was produced, for example from Combe Down. This stone lends itself particularly well to ornamental work, and indeed was widely exported for this purpose.

The great wool churches of the Cotswolds, built in the Perpendicular style, date mainly from the fifteenth century. Some of the best examples can be found at Chipping Campden, Winchcombe, Northleach and Wotton-under-Edge. Their ornamented square towers are a characteristic focal point in the Cotswold landscape, although spires are also found, for example at Painswick and Tetbury.

However, it is the high quality of the domestic architecture that is most unusual. The Cotswold vernacular style is deceptively simple [11]: a steep roof of limestone slates, pitched at 50° or more; a parapetted gable with finials; dormer windows in subsidiary gables; stone mullions, rectangular dripstones and leaded lights; and four-centred arches over the doorways. Although it is a formal, parallel style, it lends itself to variations. In the larger houses more extravagant features such as decorated doorways, curved gables and coats of arms can be found in Gothic, Renaissance and Queen Anne styles, while smaller and later houses may be more plain. Ashlar is used at least for the front walls, even of cottages, and the overall effect is one of elegant refinement. Farm buildings – especially barns – are also very fine.

Limestone roofing slates are a special feature. They are formed by exposing the laminated stone from certain areas such as Stonesfield, near Charlbury, to a hard frost and are subsequently split and trimmed – a highly skilled job. Because they are not absolutely flat, a steeply pitched roof, to prevent rain driving in, is needed.

The character of the towns and villages varies somewhat from north to south. In the north, which is generally more rural, the Cotswold vernacular style predominates. Rows of town houses and cottages face directly onto the street, sometimes clustering around a market cross or green. Their roofs and gables provide a varied skyline, while to the rear are found more cottages, roads, lanes, orchards and gardens.

In the south, the stone is generally lighter in colour and includes the silvery white of Painswick and the cream of Bath stone. Settlements are more urbanised, and there is a higher proportion of later dwellings, from sophisticated Georgian and Palladian town houses to eighteenth and nineteenth century terraces and villas.

Throughout the area, though, the building stone has a particular brightness and warmth, and there is a special sense of visual accord between the stone buildings and the surrounding fields and hillsides. All of the buildings are of the same local material, and everywhere there is moss, lichen and lush plant growth, so that whole villages seem to merge into the landscape.

3. Perceptions of the Cotswolds through time

The derivation of the name

The boundaries of the Cotswolds today are broadly defined to include the area of oolitic limestone extending from Bath to Edge Hill. However, the name originally applied to a much smaller area: the high wolds between Winchcombe and Stow-on-the-Wold. It was derived [12] not only from the Anglo-Saxon for 'high, open land', but also from Cod, the name of a Saxon chief who settled in the area. The valley land became 'Cod's dene' or 'Cutsdean' and the hill country above became 'Cotswold'. As time passed, the name also came to be used for the south of the region.

Early perceptions

There are few records of how early visitors to the Cotswolds perceived the area. Prior to the nineteenth century there were probably comparatively few travellers, and most visitors came not because they enjoyed the scene but on business. For example, the abbots travelled between their abbeys and manors at sheep-shearing and harvest; merchants came to buy wool; drovers brought cattle from Wales along the green lanes towards the London market; and pedlars and other itinerants travelled the Cotswold ridgeway. From the journals and letters of such travellers it seems likely that, like other remote, hilly and sparsely populated areas, the Cotswolds were seen as somewhat wild and untamed. Indeed, until at least the sixteenth century, this may have been the general perception of landscape and open space [13]. Kenneth Clark [14] makes the point that the medieval mind saw nature as hostile and dwelt on its horrors rather than its beauties, seeking safety rather than wilderness.

The great travellers of the late seventeenth and eighteenth centuries, on the whole, ignored the Cotswolds. Celia Fiennes, who travelled much of England on horseback, recording her experiences in her diaries, and who was raised at Broughton Castle near Banbury, favoured the lowland enclosed landscapes and paid little attention to the Cotswolds on her journeys. The Cotswolds are known to have been visited by Daniel Defoe on one of his tours, but his main interest was in the cloth industry rather than the scenery. Alexander Pope, at the same period, expressed appreciation of the pleasures of Cirencester Park but was preoccupied with Lord Bathurst's 'improvement' plans, including enclosures, follies and ambitious planting proposals.

The nineteenth century

The early nineteenth century view of the Cotswolds was most clearly expressed by William Cobbett in 1830:

"The Wold is in itself an ugly country. The soil is what is called a stone brash below, with a reddish earth mixed with little bits of this brash at top, and... is very shallow; and, as fields are divided by walls made of this brash, and, as there are, for

Countryside around Dixton Manor *c. 1730, British School, Anon (Cheltenham Art Gallery and Museums, Gloucestershire / Bridgeman Art Library).*

A Cotswold Walk: *Painswick from the South c. 1920, Charles Gere (John Gere).*

St Martin's Summer *1915, Sir William Rothenstein* (*The Manchester City Art Galleries*).

A Cotswold farm *1928, Paul Fripp* (*Cheltenham Art Gallery and Museums, Gloucestershire / Bridgeman Art Library*).

Haytime in the Cotswolds *1939, James Bateman* (*Southampton City Art Gallery*).

a mile or two together, no trees to be seen, and as the surface is not smooth and green like the downs, this is a sort of country, having less to please the eye than any other that I have ever seen, always save and except the heaths like those of Bagshot and Hindhead. Yet, even this Wold has many fertile dells in it, and sends out, from its highest parts, several streams, each of which has its pretty valley and meadows [15]."

Accounting for this lack of interest is not easy, but at least two factors appear to have been at work. Cobbett himself refers to the lack of trees, which at that time were generally considered to be an indispensable adjunct of attractive rural scenery. Lack of patronage may have been another factor. In the early nineteenth century the arbiters of taste were the rural landowning aristocracy, who saw little demand for descriptions of villages and domestic rural architecture.

Later in the century these factors began to change. The prejudice against open scenery began to break down, as moors and fells became more popular. Rising urban middle classes became interested in discovering and displaying their rural origins. Thus, throughout the country, the village became a major subject in rural painting.

At the forefront of this change of opinion was William Morris, who came to live at Kelmscot, near Lechlade, in 1871. Morris 'discovered' the Cotswold vernacular architecture and promoted its conservation through his writings and by founding the Society for the Protection of Ancient Buildings. His work had repercussions among the wide circle of artists, craftsmen and writers associated with him. It laid the foundations for the Arts and Crafts movement, which investigated and revived old English traditions, vernacular architecture, cottage gardens and folk music. For this purpose, the Cotswolds were ideal.

The twentieth century

From the turn of the century the Arts and Crafts movement was particularly strongly represented in the Cotswolds with the Guild of Handicrafts being set up in Chipping Campden. In 1903 C R Ashbee, the Guild's founder, wrote of the 'simplicity and beauty which constitute the chief interest of Cotswold building' [16]. In 1906 the architect Sir Edwin Lutyens bought and had restored the village of Upper Slaughter. Elsewhere, much credit for early conservation of the buildings must go to the artist F L Griggs RA, at Chipping Campden; and to the group of architects at Sapperton, including Ernest and Sidney Barnsley and Norman Jewson.

At the same time, the area's popularity with painters, musicians and poets blossomed. John Singer Sargent was at the centre of an American colony of artists at Broadway; and other painters such as Alfred East, William Rothenstein, Charles Gere, H F Bateman and Paul Fripp produced landscape, village and farm scenes that brought the Cotswolds to the attention of a wide audience. The local folk music was written down by Cecil Sharp in the 1920s at Bledington, and Vaughan Williams, from Down Ampney, wrote *The Lark Ascending*. The setting for the music is the wolds, and the effect is intended to be 'of a lark flying above a landscape as varied as that glowing region' [17]. The Gloucestershire poets Leonard Clark, Frank Mansell,

Ivor Gurney and others also wrote about the area.

By the 1920s the Cotswolds had risen to mass popularity as the classic region of the English vernacular, and this is reflected in writings about the region. The themes stressed are timelessness, the virtues of the rural way of life and the visual unity of landscape and architecture. For example, in the 1940s H J Massingham wrote:

"It is only on Cotswold, I think, that one lives with the past without feeling it to be a museum piece. Everything is mixed up on the Cotswolds – nature and the works of man and the periods in which he executed them. Yet the result is not confusion but unity [18]."

Slightly later, Robert Bryan was prompted to write of the Cotswolds that:

"The peace you will find there is the peace of unhurried toil. There is plenty doing, but it is done without fret or fuss, storm or controversy, against a background of years and centuries in which the inhabitants have won their living from the land, unharmed by urban incursions [19]."

In other words, the area came to be seen as a pastoral retreat, 'a world that is rare, precious, vanishing' [13], as portrayed in Laurie Lee's *Cider with Rosie* (set at Slad, near Stroud):

"Living down there was like living in a bean-pod; one could see nothing but the bed one lay in. Most of the cottages were built of Cotswold stone and were roofed by split-stone tiles. The tiles grew a kind of golden moss which sparkled like crystallised honey. Behind the cottages were long steep gardens full of cabbages, fruit bushes, roses, rabbit hutches, earth closets, bicycles and pigeon-lofts [20]."

Perceptions of the Cotswolds today

From as early as the 1940s and 1950s, recognition of the Cotswolds' outstanding scenic and cultural qualities gave rise to widespread public care and concern about landscape conservation. Moves began to be made to protect the area from development pressures. For example, the Council for the Protection of Rural England was first founded, and active, in the Cotswolds; and from the 1960s there were strict controls on choice of building materials.

Today a wide range of public bodies, amenity societies and special interest groups work together towards the area's conservation and management, under the auspices of the Joint Advisory Committee for the Cotswolds AONB.

The area continues to be immensely popular, both as a tourist and a day-trip destination as is evident, not least, from the plethora of books and guides about the area. This popularity reflects, in part, the proximity of the Cotswolds to large, highly mobile urban populations; and the high value that those populations tend to place upon the rural way of life. More importantly, though, it reflects the Cotswolds' national and international reputation as the quintessential English landscape. Indeed, the Cotswolds have come to be regarded as the hallmark of much modern landscape and architectural taste.

4. Landscape change

As the purpose of the AONB designation is to conserve the natural beauty of the landscape, it is important to have an appreciation of how the Cotswold landscape has changed in the recent past, and how it may change in future. Are these changes likely to threaten its landscape character and qualities?

Landscape change this century

There is surprisingly little detailed documentary evidence about recent landscape change in the Cotswolds. The following information, derived mainly from secondary sources, suggests how the landscape may have changed since 1900.

In agricultural terms the main change has been an increase in the proportion of arable land at the expense of permanent pasture. Most of this change appears to have taken place during the last fifty years on the upland plateau and dip slope. In 1935, it was recorded that 40–42 per cent of the Cotswolds was covered by permanent (largely unimproved) grassland, whereas in 1983, the figure was only 2 per cent [8]. Vast areas of lighter land were brought under the plough for the first time, and mainly put down to cereals. Visually, this has probably had quite a dramatic effect upon the landscape, as large areas of traditional sheep walk have disappeared to be replaced by ploughed fields and grain.

In parallel with the increase in arable land, sheep rearing declined, and intensive rearing of beef and dairy cattle grew. The expansion in cattle rearing was accompanied by grassland improvement, and the making of silage rather than hay. More intensive techniques also led to the construction of new farm buildings and the loss of field boundaries (both hedges and drystone walls). Hedgerow loss took place mainly during the 1960s and 1970s; it seems to have slowed or stopped during the 1980s. Loss of drystone walls continues, however. This is partly because the oolites, unlike other more resistant walling stones, weather and shatter. Many of the Cotswolds' drystone walls were built during the eighteenth and nineteenth century enclosures: they are now in need not only of maintenance, but also of replacement.

Perhaps somewhat surprisingly the area of woodland in the Cotswolds appears to have changed very little this century. Evidence [9] suggests that although there was significant loss of semi-natural ancient woodlands during the nineteenth century, since the 1920s only 3.4 per cent of ancient woodland has been lost, mainly to agriculture.

However, there has been a clear change in woodland character, as 47 per cent of the ancient woodland area has been replanted and converted to intensive forestry since 1900 [9]. Most of this change occurred in the period 1960–80, during which extensive conifer plantations were introduced; hence, many ancient woodland sites now have only small areas of semi-natural woodland remaining. During the same period the dip slope landscape, in particular, changed in character due to Dutch elm disease.

Changes in agriculture have brought damage and destruction to other semi-natural habitats. In some areas commons have been lost, and in others they have been invaded by scrub, due to the reduction in sheep grazing. The limestone grasslands, once so common, have become a scarce resource; streams and marshes have been damaged by agricultural run-off, abstraction of river and ground waters, drainage of wet meadows and clearance of marginal vegetation.

Change due to building development has been held fairly firmly in check by strict development control throughout the Cotswolds. Pressures, particularly for residential and tourist development, first became evident as early as the 1930s and have tended to be concentrated in those villages close to major road or rail through-routes. In some of these villages, despite strict development control, new building has had a detrimental 'suburbanising' effect upon the landscape. This manifests itself not only in reconstituted stone and non-vernacular architectural features such as shallow roofs and picture windows, but also in street layouts and planting. For example, modern houses are set back from the street in gardens, whereas traditional Cotswold town houses and cottages form a continuous street frontage. Ornamental shrub and conifer planting around new housing often takes the place of traditional cottage gardens. Other building development, fortunately, has been fairly limited, although major new roads, quarries, pylons, radio masts and airfields, such as Colerne airfield, cause localised visual intrusion.

In places, tourism has caused direct pressures on the landscape, although they are still not as serious as in some other parts of the country, such as the Lake District. For example, on every sunny Sunday throughout the year, Bourton-on-the-Water, Bibury and other popular villages suffer tremendous congestion while on sites such as Painswick Beacon and Cleeve Common erosion caused by walkers, riders and motorcyclists may scar the hillside. Ironically, elsewhere in the Cotswolds, other equally charming villages and beauty spots are little known and seldom visited.

Forces for future landscape change

Future landscape change is difficult to predict with any certainty, but the most likely forces for change can be identified.

Further agricultural intensification is now unlikely, at least in the short term, due to set-aside and farm diversification. Evidence to date suggests that the take-up rate for set-aside in the Cotswold counties is likely to be fairly high. Unfortunately, though, set-aside will not enable the re-establishment of traditional Cotswold sheep walks, because the scheme precludes grazing on fallow land. It should assist in the retention and management of hedgerows, but it will not lead to the renewal of drystone walls.

Top Left; Tourism has a major impact on popular villages such as Bourton-on-the-Water. Considerable problems arise from the volume of visitors at peak periods.

Top Middle; In certain areas erosion by walkers, riders and motorcyclists may scar the hillside. The example shown is Haresfield Hill, north of Stroud.

Top Right; Many of the Cotswold drystone walls are now in need of replacement. Unlike more resistant walling stones, the oolites weather and shatter.

Left; Encouragement to other attractions, together with a detailed visitor management strategy will help to relieve 'honey pot' areas such as Dundas on the Kennet and Avon Canal (Photo © Martin Brown/British Waterways).

Above; There is the potential, over a number of years, for infill and peripheral development to overwhelm existing towns and villages, and to creep up valley sides. Wotton-under-Edge has already been affected.

Top Middle; In future, built development is likely to be the most important force for landscape change. Even the most sensitive farm building conversion brings social change and a new appearance of affluence.

Top Right; The existence of reserves brings changes to the landscape as quarrying can affect large areas.

Right; The conversion since the 1930s, of large areas of traditional sheep walk to arable land, has had a dramatic effect upon the landscape.

It is likely that there will be new pressures for afforestation as farmers are encouraged to plant trees through set-aside and the woodland grant scheme. This is not necessarily a threat, provided that the new planting is consistent with the existing landscape character. For example, on the scarp and valley slopes, planting that does not follow the natural landform is likely to be visually disruptive, while on the high wold plateau, insensitively sited large-scale planting could close off important views and destroy the unique open character of the scenery. Care will also need to be taken in species choice. Extensive use of conifers, particularly on ancient woodland sites, would be inappropriate to the Cotswold character. If these pitfalls can be avoided, however, new afforestation may bring visual and recreational benefits.

The future of existing woodlands and shelterbelts is by no means assured. Although their clearance for agriculture is unlikely, many of the woodlands, particularly the beech woodlands of the scarp, are now mature or over-mature, and in need of regeneration. A comprehensive, phased regeneration programme is needed – otherwise large areas may have to be clear-felled and replanted.

With regard to building development, continued vigilance is required. There is evidence that with growing congestion in the urban areas of the south-east, people are increasingly returning to rural areas. Coupled with further growth in second homes, and increased demand for tourist accommodation, this seems certain to result in additional development pressures. Agricultural diversification and the encouragement of rural tourism may accentuate the pressures. As in the past, they are likely to be concentrated near the transport corridors which facilitate commuting and general access. For example, the M40 extension is likely to bring new development to the north-east Cotswolds and Edge Hill.

The result will probably be a growing number of applications to convert farm buildings to other uses, as well as applications for new infill building. Although farm building conversions can have a positive effect, by providing funds for restoration, they have a subtle, cumulative landscape impact, by bringing social change and a new appearance of affluence. Infill development poses even greater risks: gradually, over a number of years, it has the potential to overwhelm existing towns and villages and to creep up valley sides, encroaching visually upon surrounding countryside.

Congestion and erosion due to sheer visitor numbers also seem set to increase in 'honeypot' villages, along the escarpment and in certain other areas such as along the Kennet and Avon Canal. Much more attention will need to be given to managing pressures at these sites. Pressures may be relieved further by directing visitors to other areas, for example by opening up new sites of interest such as the cloth mills of the 'Golden Valley'.

Other forms of development must also be very carefully controlled, designed and managed. Although major proposals have been comparatively rare in the past, they do occur. In particular, there are a number of major road schemes in the pipeline at present, which could potentially bring significant landscape changes to the Cotswolds. These include improvements to the A417 at Crickley Hill; the proposed A46 Batheaston bypass; and a further road scheme for the Limpley Stoke valley. All of these proposals are visually highly sensitive.

Elsewhere, minerals and landfill could bring changes. For instance, in some areas near Bath, limestone quarrying continues and there are known to be extensive reserves of Fuller's Earth. Planning applications for waste disposal within the region are not uncommon.

Finally, the landscape of the Cotswolds is specially sensitive to the introduction of large new structures on high ground. Thus any new radio mast, defence system or transmission line proposals could have adverse impacts.

A threat to landscape quality?

The conclusion of this review of landscape change is that, compared to many other areas of the countryside, the Cotswolds have altered fairly little over the last century. The most important change has been the dramatic conversion from pasture to arable, with consequent loss of sheep walks. Also noticeable have been the loss of stone walls; the change in woodland character; and the 'suburbanisation' of certain villages. On the whole, though, major impacts on scenic quality have been resisted. Most changes have been relatively slow, local and small-scale.

Future scenic change, too, is likely to be gradual and cumulative, on the whole. Landscape is the product of interactions between natural and human influences over many centuries. There can and should be no question of 'fossilising' it in its present form. On the other hand, there is a need to be aware of the 'key' qualities of the landscape, and to assess how they are most vulnerable to change, so that appropriate action can be taken. These issues are examined in the final chapter.

5. The importance of the Cotswold landscape

The importance of a landscape is hard to measure. It depends upon a multitude of factors, not least of which is personal preference. Nonetheless, it is now widely accepted that it is possible to give a reliable assessment of landscape value on the basis of 'informed opinion, the trained eye, and common sense' [3]. This approach was recommended by the Inspector at the public inquiry into the North Pennines AONB designation in 1985, and has since been formally adopted by the Countryside Commission. It is an approach which has been used in the preparation of this report.

The purpose of this chapter is to identify and highlight the outstanding qualities of the Cotswold landscape. The intention is to make explicit the reasons why the designation was originally made, and – in general terms – why it is now proposed that it should be extended.

It is also hoped that it will provide additional guidance to the work of the fourteen local authorities who have the major responsibility for implementing the designation and management of the area. The local authorities concerned, together with nine amenity and special interest organisations, form the Joint Advisory Committee for the Cotswolds AONB. The Committee's function is to help ensure the preparation, coordination and implementation of positive countryside management policies for the whole area [21].

Outstanding qualities

There is wide acceptance, through the existing AONB designation, that the Cotswolds are an area of outstanding scenic qualities. This is confirmed by our field surveys, by factual evidence, and by people's perceptions as expressed through painting, music, literature and the conservation movement. There are at least four sets of qualities that make the Cotswold landscape outstanding: its remarkable visual unity; its unique vernacular architecture; its reputation as a rural idyll; and its local scenic diversity.

Visual unity

Nowhere in Britain has the underlying rock had such a dominant and unifying effect on the landscape and architecture as in the Cotswolds. As a result, topography, vegetation and settlement are uniquely blended and in harmony. This unity is emphasised by the recurrent visual themes of stone walls, sheep walks and wolds; ancient beech woods; hill forts and Roman roads; woollen towns and cottage gardens; manor houses and parks; water mills and water meadows. It is reinforced by the visually dominant scarp and the Jurassic Ridgeway that stretch the full length of the area. Most of all, though, it is seen in the fact that entire villages and whole small towns are constructed of nothing but oolitic limestone, with not a brick or slate in sight.

This quality of visual unity is underlined time and again in writings about the Cotswolds. It is summarised well by David Verey:

"The colour is generally warmer in the north Cotswolds and greyer in the south; but everywhere it seems to have the quality of retaining light, and responding to the moods of the day.... Everywhere the stone buildings achieve a visual accord with the landscape [22]."

Unique vernacular architecture

For many people, the villages of the Cotswolds are the epitome of English vernacular architecture, the 'village show-pieces of England' [11]. Indeed, some consider that the landscape takes second place. For example, Alec Clifton-Taylor says that:

"Whereas our vernacular buildings are usually mere incidents in their landscape settings, albeit often agreeable ones, in the Cotswolds the buildings themselves, even the barns, are of such high quality that at every turn, it is they that we notice first [11]."

In even the most humble dwellings, the standard of workmanship is extraordinarily high, and the building style is so simple and classic that is it still copied throughout the limestone belt several centuries later. The building materials, too, are special: not only the dressed ashlar stone walls, but also the distinctive limestone roofing slates that add 'the crowning touch of harmony, in colour and in texture, with the surrounding landscape' [11]. The common use of these materials has meant that even when the basic Gothic style was altered and ornamented to suit the fashion of later periods, its essential Cotswold character remained.

The vernacular architecture of the Cotswold villages is complemented by their fine gardens. There are many famous gardens such as Hidcote, but of equal if not greater importance are the colourful cottage gardens that spill over banks and walls, where they are shown to best advantage against the local stone. The high standard of care and attention given to architecture and gardens alike is, in itself, quite unusual.

Rural idyll

The Cotswolds' reputation as a rural idyll is now deeply rooted in the modern psyche. It is related partly to the Cotswolds' long history of habitation, which has been particularly well explored and documented by archaeologists and historians. It is also linked to twentieth century perceptions of the area as a place where time has stood still, and where it is possible to re-establish age-old links between nature and humanity. This concept was comparatively new and esoteric in the 1920s: today, with growing concern about environmental problems, it is widespread, and this is one of the main reasons why the Cotswolds is such a highly valued landscape, both nationally and internationally.

One of the Cotswold's outstanding landscape features is the harmony between topography, vegetation and settlement.

This pastoral quality comes across particularly well in the writings of Laurie Lee about his childhood home at Slad:

"The valley was narrow, steep and almost entirely cut off; it was also a funnel for winds, a channel for the floods, and a jungly, bird crammed, insect-hopping suntrap whenever there happened to be any sun. Like an island, it was possessed of curious survivals – rare orchids and Roman snails.... The sides of the valley were rich in pasture and the crests heavily covered in beech woods [20]."

Scenic diversity

There can be few areas with the physical, geological and visual unity of the Cotswolds that are yet so diverse scenically. Although this may sound a contradiction in terms, it is not. Within the long limestone belt there are immense contrasts in the scenery at local level. The scarp is linear in aspect and dominated by woodlands, commons and hill forts, behind which the incised landscapes form complex, lush scenic 'fjords'. The high wold is characterised by the clean lines of its rolling spacious plateaux, which contrast strongly with the intimate, bosky valleys and villages; whereas the dip slope has wide open skies and water meadows. Throughout the area, the grandeur of the views from the ridges and plateaux into the valleys below is quite unmatched. There is a mix of habitat types, from ancient beech woodland to limestone grassland, and this adds local visual and ecological interest. Building materials and styles, too, differ markedly from south to north.

The overall effect is one of immense scenic diversity, with many individual features of special historical, ecological and architectural value.

Vulnerability to change

Together these qualities make the Cotswolds an outstanding landscape. Although there are few immediate and dramatic landscape threats, there are nonetheless some trends which, if allowed to become established, could lead to fundamental alterations in the appearance of valued scenic features.

In our view the following changes have already had an adverse effect on the landscape of the Cotswolds AONB:

● conversion of traditional sheep walks and limestone grasslands to arable land;

● the continuing deterioration and loss of drystone walls from plateau areas;

● replanting of ancient semi-natural woodlands as coniferous or mixed plantations;

● 'suburbanisation' of some villages, hamlets and farmsteads by inappropriate new development.

Where possible, action should be taken to halt or reverse these trends through grants, incentives and other appropriate measures.

In future, the most important threats to landscape quality are likely to be:

● new afforestation that is out of keeping with the Cotswold landscape character because of its location, configuration or species composition;

● poor design quality and detailing of building conversions and infill developments;

● excessive expansion of existing towns and villages with developments that bring social change and do not respect the character of traditional Cotswold buildings and gardens;

● new developments such as caravan sites and farm attractions associated with agricultural diversification and farm tourism;

● increased congestion and erosion in the vicinity of key tourist attractions;

● insensitive new road schemes;

● other visually intrusive developments such as quarrying, landfill and transmission lines, that may be proposed in certain areas.

Of this list of potential threats, building developments and road schemes will probably prove the most serious.

This analysis suggests, in turn, the following key conservation issues that are likely to come to the fore:

● how to encourage the reinstatement of the upland sheep walk landscape, with its limestone grasslands and drystone walls;

● how to direct and guide new afforestation to ensure optimum landscape and recreational benefit;

● how to achieve phased regeneration of the mature beech woodlands of the scarp;

● how to control and where possible accommodate appropriate new development into the Cotswold villages without damaging their vernacular character;

● how to direct tourism pressures away from sensitive villages and sites to other parts of the Cotswolds, and manage the sites where congestion occurs;

● how to achieve essential road and other infrastructure development in areas of the utmost landscape sensitivity.

Many of these issues are already being addressed by landowners, the local authorities, and other organisations with specialist interests in the countryside. For example, the Joint Advisory Committee for the Cotswolds AONB has coordinated the implementation of a development control code of practice, and is soon to introduce guidelines for new woodland planting.

However, it is clear that in future these and other conservation issues will require increased effort and attention from all those who have a concern for the Cotswold countryside.

6. Conclusion

The Cotswolds are of outstanding importance as one of the finest English historic rural landscapes, a hallmark of modern architectural and landscape taste. Their geology, topography and history of successive prehistoric, Roman and especially medieval settlement have clearly influenced the development of the landscape. Throughout both the existing AONB, and the larger area now proposed for designation by the Countryside Commission, there are distinct visual, ecological and architectural characteristics. Since the late nineteenth century, the area has come to be valued highly for the fine craftsmanship found in its buildings, for its folk history and for its rural way of life. Its outstanding landscape qualities are its visual unity; its unique vernacular architecture; its reputation as a rural idyll; and its immense scenic diversity.

In the words of Robert Bryan:

> "Nowhere in all England is there such a lack of stridency. The colours, the grey of the stone walls which over much of this land do duty for hedges, and of the cottages and manor houses, the green and pale gold of the pasture and arable fields, seem softly blended....The landscape is a watercolour... [22]."

References

1. *Wildlife and Countryside Act 1981*, Section 53 (2), Her Majesty's Stationary Office, 1981.

2. Countryside Commission, *Landscape Assessment: A Countryside Commission Approach*, CCD18, Countryside Commission, 1987.

3. Countryside Commission, *Areas of Outstanding Natural Beauty: A Policy Statement*, CCP157, Countryside Commission, 1983.

4. Murray, J W and Hawkins, A B ,'Geology and Physical Environment', in C and A M Hadfield (eds), *The Cotswolds: A New Study*, David and Charles, 1973.

5. Rackham, O, *The History of the Countryside*, Dent, 1986.

6. Smith, I F, Eagles, B N and Morgan, K, 'From Prehistory to AD 1500', in C and A M Hadfield (eds), *The Cotswolds: A New Study*, David and Charles, 1973.

7. Hoskins, W G, *The Making of the English Landscape*, Penguin, 1970.

8. Joint Advisory Committee for the Cotswolds Area of Outstanding Natural Beauty, *Nature Conservation: Countryside Management* (unpublished), 1983.

9. Bullard, P (ed), *A Revised Inventory of Gloucestershire's Ancient Woodlands: The Cotswold Plateau*, Gloucestershire Trust for Nature Conservation, 1987.

10. Penoyre, J and Penoyre, J, *Houses in the Landscape: A Regional Study of Vernacular Building Styles in England and Wales*, Faber, 1984.

11. Clifton-Taylor, A, *The Pattern of English Building*, 4th edition, Faber, 1987.

12. Smith, A H (ed), *The Place Names of Gloucestershire, Part 1, English Place Names Society*, vol 38, Cambridge University Press, 1964.

13. Drabble, M, *A Writer's Britain: Landscape in Literature*, Thames and Hudson, 1979.

14. Clark, K, *Landscape Into Art*, John Murray, 1949.

15. Cobbett, W C, *Rural Rides*, Penguin , 1967.

16. Ashbee, C R, 'The Guild of Handicrafts at Chipping Campden', *The Art Journal*, 1903.

17. Burke, J, *Musical Landscapes*, Webb and Bower, 1983.

18. Massingham, H J, 'The Cotswolds', in S P B Mais and T Stephenson (eds), *Lovely Britain*, Odhams, 1945.

19. Bryan, R, *The British Countryside in Colour*, Odhams, 1950.

20. Lee, L, *Cider with Rosie*, Hogarth, 1959.

21. Joint Advisory Committee for the Cotswolds Area of Outstanding Natural Beauty, *Countryside Management: Background Report* (unpublished), 1982.

22. Verey, D, 'Architecture' in C and A M Hadfield (eds), *The Cotswolds: A New Study*, David and Charles, 1973.

The Cotswolds – a landscape of contrasts.